REVISED

CHARTER

(AS AMENDED,)

OF THE

CITY OF DETROIT.

PUBLISHED BY ORDER OF

COMMON COUNCIL.

DETROIT:
W. F. STOREY, PRINTER TO CITY.
1859.

REVISED CITY CHARTER.

CHAPTER I.

INCORPORATION—CITY AND WARD BOUNDARIES.

SECTION 1. *The People of the State of Michigan enact*, That the corporation heretofore created and now known as Corporation. "The Mayor, Recorder, Aldermen and Freemen of the City of Detroit," shall be and continue to be a corporation by the name of "The City of Detroit," and by that name may sue and be sued, implead and be impleaded, complain and defend, in any court of record and any other place whatsoever; may have a common seal and alter it at pleasure, and may take, hold, purchase, lease, convey and dispose of any real, personal or mixed estate for the use of said corporation.

SEC. 2. The district of country in the county of Wayne and State of Michigan, hereinafter particularly described, is hereby constituted and declared to be a city, by the name of Detroit, and subject to the municipal government of said corporation, said district of country being bounded as follows, Boundaries. viz.: Beginning at a point on the national boundary line in the Detroit River, directly opposite and in a line with the dividing line between the Baker and Woodbridge Farms, so called, and running thence north twenty-two degrees and forty-seven minutes west, to the margin of said river; thence north twenty-two degrees and forty-seven minutes west, along said dividing line to the rear or northerly line of the Baker Farm aforesaid; thence north-easterly along the rear or northerly line of the Baker, Labrosse and Forsyth Farms, so called, to the north-westerly corner of the Jones Farm, so called; thence north sixty degrees east, on a course parallel with Jefferson Avenue, to a point opposite the dividing line between the Dequindre and Witherell Farms, so called; thence south twenty-six degrees east, to the north-easterly corner of the Dequindre Farm aforesaid, being the north-western corner of the Witherell Farm aforesaid; thence south twenty-six degrees east, along said line of said farms, to the margin of the Detroit River aforesaid; thence south twenty-six degrees east to the national boundary line in said river, and thence south-westerly along said national boundary line to the place of beginning. The wards of said city shall be and remain as heretofore laid out and constituted, until altered by the Common Council of said city, as authorized by this act. (*See Appendix.*)

CHAPTER II.

OFFICERS—WHO ELECTED, WHO APPOINTED, QUALIFICATIONS, BONDS, OFFICIAL TERMS, REMOVAL, VACANCY.

Officers elected on general ticket.

SECTION 1. The following officers of the corporation shall be elected at the annual city election, on a general ticket, by the qualified electors of the whole city, viz.: Mayor, Recorder, City Clerk, Attorney, Treasurer, Marshal, City Surveyor, and Director of the Poor.

On ward ticket.

The following officers of the corporation shall be elected at said election on a ward ticket, in each ward, by the qualified electors thereof, viz.: Two Aldermen, two School Inspectors, a Collector, Overseer of Highways, and Constable.

Officers appointed by Common Council.

SEC. 2. The following officers shall be appointed by the Common Council, at a meeting to be held on the second Tuesday of January in each year, viz.: Superintendent of Alms-House, a Sealer of Weights and Measures, a Clerk of the Recorder's Court, who shall be appointed on the recommendation of the Recorder, one or more Collectors, one or more Physicians, one or more Street Commissioners, one or more Assistant Marshals, one or more Clerks of Markets, and such other officers, deputies, assistant officers and agents, whose appointment shall be authorized by prior resolution of the Common Council. A Controller shall be appointed on the second Tuesday of March, preceding the expiration of his term of office. Controller.

SEC. 3. There shall also be the following board of officers of the corporation, viz.: a Board of Water Commissioners, to be appointed and constituted as provided for in the act incorporating "The Board of Water Commissioners of the City of Detroit," approved February 14th, 1853 ; a Board of Education, to be constituted as provided for in the act incorporating "The Board of Education of the City of Detroit," approved February 17th, 1842, and all acts amendatory thereto; and a Board of Inspectors of Election, to be appointed and constituted as hereinafter provided ; and a Board of three Sewer Commissioners, who shall be appointed by the Common Council, on the nomination of the Mayor, and who shall appoint a competent engineer, and, with his aid, it shall be their duty to propose a plan for constructing sewers and drains for the whole city—having reference, however, to the sewers and drains already constructed, or in process of construction—and said Board shall have such further powers and duties, in respect to the sewers and drains of said city, as said Common Council shall by ordinance prescribe. Said Commissioners shall receive no compensation for their services, shall hold their office for the term of five years, with the exception of the first Board, who shall hold their office for the respective terms of three, four, and five years, and the respective terms of each shall be determined by lot, under the direction of the City Attorney and Controller, and when thus determined, such determination shall be certified by said Attorney and Controller to the Common Council, and entered upon their journal, and such certificate shall be evidence of the respective term for which the several mem-

Board of Water Commissioners.

Board of Education.

Board of Inspectors of Election.

Sewer Commissioners.

Engineer.

Sewers and Drains.

Commissioners to receive no compensation.

Term of Office.

Duties of Engineer.

bers of said Board have been elected. It shall be the duty of said engineer, under the direction of said Board, to superintend the construction and repair of sewers.

Justices of the Peace—their term of office, jurisdiction, powers and duties

SEC. 4. There shall be six Justices of the Peace in and for said city, who shall be elected on the general ticket at the annual city election in the same manner, shall hold their offices for the same terms and by the same tenure, possess the same jurisdiction and powers, subject to the act of the Legislature establishing a Police Court of the City of Detroit, and be subject to the same duties and liabilities, as provided by the general laws of this State in relation to the election, jurisdiction, powers, duties and liabilities of Justices of the Peace for townships: but the Justices of the Peace of said city, now in office, shall continue to hold their offices for the terms for which they have been elected, and in conformity to the general laws of this State: *Provided, however*, That at the election, to be held in April, 1857, a Justice of the Peace may be elected to fill the vacancy which will occur by the expiration of the term of such Justice in July, 1857.

Justices now in office to continue.

Proviso.

Officers to be residents of Detroit.

SEC. 5. No person shall be elected or appointed to, or shall hold, any office under this act, who shall not be at the time of his election, or appointment, and so long as he shall hold such office, a resident elector of said city; and no person shall be elected or appointed to, or shall hold office for any ward in said city, who at the time of his election or appointment, and so long as he shall hold such office, shall not be a resident elector of the ward from and for which he may be elected or appointed. If any person, elected or appointed to any office of the corporation, shall cease to be a resident of the city, or of the ward, for which he may have been elected or appointed, such office shall thereby be vacated: *Provided, however*, That a School Inspector shall not vacate his office by his removal from one ward to another ward in said city.

Proviso.

Qualificati'ns of Attorney.

SEC. 6. No person shall be elected to the office of Attorney, unless he be at the time of his election a Counsellor of the Supreme Court of this State of two years' standing.

SEC. 7. No person shall be elected or appointed to any office created by this act, who is now, or hereafter may be, a defaulter to said city, or to any board of officers thereof, or to the State of Michigan, or any county thereof; and any person shall be considered a defaulter who has refused, or neglected, or may hereafter refuse or neglect, for thirty days after demand made, to account for and pay over to the party authorized to receive the same, any public money which has come in his possession. If any person holding any such office shall become a defaulter, while in office, the same shall thereby be vacated.

Defaulters ineligible.

SEC. 8. No person shall be elected or appointed to any office under this act, except the office of Scavenger and Chimney Sweeper, unless he is able to read and write the English language intelligibly; and if any such person be elected or appointed, the Common Council shall declare such appointment or election void.

Ignorance a disqualification for office

SEC. 9. No member of the Common Council shall, after his election and during the time for which he was elected, or within one year thereafter, be appointed to any office under this act, which shall have been created, or the emoluments of which shall have been increased, during such time.

Aldermen to hold no other office.

SEC. 10. No person interested directly or indirectly, either as principal or surety, in any contract or agreement, written or verbal, to which the corporation shall be a party in interest, or to which any officer or board under this act shall officially be a party, for the construction of any sewer, pavement, building, or performance of any public work whatever, or for involving the expenditure, receipt or disposition of money or property of the corporation, Common Council, or by any officer or board under this act, shall be eligible or appointed to any office under this act; and if any person thus interested shall be elected or appointed to office, his election, or appointment, shall be void, and his office shall be deemed vacant.

Persons interested disqualified for office.

Officers becoming interested to be removed.

SEC. 11. If any member of the Common Council or other officer of the corporation, after his election or appointment, or while in office, shall become, or cause himself to become, interested, directly or indirectly, in any contract or agreement, written or verbal, to which the corporation shall be a party in interest, or to which any officer or board under this act shall officially be a party, or in any question, subject or proceeding, pending before the Common Council, with intent to gain, directly or indirectly, any benefit, profit, or pecuniary advantage, he shall be removed from his office, and his office declared vacant by the Common Council, and he shall be deemed guilty of willful and corrupt malfeasance in office, and may be prosecuted therefor, and on conviction, shall be

Punishment.

punished by a fine not exceeding one thousand dollars, or imprisonment in the State prison not exceeding one year, or both, at the discretion of the Court.

SEC. 12. If any person shall offer, directly or indirectly, to a member of the Common Council, or if any member of the

Bribery.

Common Council shall directly or indirectly accept, or agree to accept, or receive any money, goods, or chattels, or any bank note, bank bill, bond, promissory note, due-bill, bill of exchange, draft, order or certificate, or any security for the payment of money or goods and chattels, or any deed or writing containing a conveyance of land, or containing a transfer of any interest in real estate, any valuable contract, in force, or any other property or reward whatsoever, in consideration that such member of the Common Council will vote affirmatively or negatively, or that he will not vote, or that he will use his interest or influence on any question, ordinance, resolution, or other matter or proceeding pending before the Common Council, he shall be removed from office, and his office declared vacant by the Common Council, and both he and the person making such offer as aforesaid, shall

Punishment.

be deemed guilty of misdemeanor, and may be prosecuted therefor, and on conviction, shall be punished by a fine not exceeding one thousand dollars, or imprisonment in the State prison not exceeding one year, or both, at the discretion of the Court.

SEC. 13. The Water Commissioners shall hold their respective offices for the term of five years, the Controller for the term of three years, the Recorder for the term of six years, the Mayor, Aldermen, School Inspectors, Treasurer, City Clerk, Attorney, Marshal, City Surveyor and Director of the Poor for the term of two years, and all other officers who are elected or appointed, shall hold for the term of one year: *Provided, however*, that all officers, whether elected or appointed, shall hold their offices respectively until their successors shall be duly elected or appointed and qualified, and shall enter upon the discharge of their duties. Terms of Office. Proviso.

SEC. 14. The official terms of all officers who are elected shall commence on the second Tuesday of January, after the annual city election at which they may have been elected, on which day there shall be a meeting of the Common Council; and the official terms of all officers who are appointed shall commence and expire on the third Tuesday of January, on which day there shall also be a meeting of the Common Council, except the Water Commissioners, whose official terms shall commence and expire as provided for in the act incorporating "The Board of Water Commissioners of the City of Detroit," approved February 14th, 1853, and the Controller, whose official term shall commence and expire on the first Tuesday in April. Commencement of Official Terms

SEC. 15. Every officer appointed or elected under this act, before entering on the duties of his office, shall take and subscribe the following oath of office: "I do solemnly swear (or affirm) that I will support the constitution of the United States and of this State, and that I will faithfully discharge the duties of such office to the best of my ability," and shall file said oath, duly certified by the officer before whom it was taken, in the office of the Clerk of the City. Oath of Office

SEC. 16. Officers, who are elected in the annual city election, shall take and subscribe the oath of office before the

Oaths, before whom taken. City Clerk, file their official bonds and enter upon their official duties on the second Tuesday of January next ensuing their election, or within ten days thereafter; and officers who are appointed for full terms, shall take and subscribe the oath of office, file their official bonds and enter upon their official duties on the third Tuesday of January, or within ten days thereafter; but officers, who are either elected at a special election, or appointed to fill the unexpired portion of a term, shall take and subscribe the oath of office, file their official bonds and enter upon their duties within ten days next ensuing notice of their election or appointment, except Justices of the Peace.

Discontinuing Office. SEC. 17. Any office hereby authorized, but not specially named, may at any time be discontinued by the Common Council, and if there be an incumbent in such office, such discontinuance shall, on notice thereof, discharge him from the office and a further execution of its duties, and his office be deemed vacant.

Recorder subject to impeachment. SEC. 18. The Recorder shall be subject to impeachment and removal from office for corrupt conduct in office, or for crimes and misdemeanors, in the same manner as judicial officers, pursuant to the provisions of the constitution of this State.

Expulsion from Office. SEC. 19. The Common Council may expel or remove from office any of its members, or any other officer holding office by election, except the Mayor and Recorder, for corrupt or willful malfeasance or misfeasance in office, or for willful neglect of the duties of his office, by a vote of two-thirds of all the Aldermen elect, and in such case the reasons for such expulsion or removal shall be entered on the records of the Common Council, with the names and votes of the members voting on the question. No officer holding office by election shall be expelled or removed by said Common Council, unless first furnished with a copy of the charges in writing, and allowed to be heard in his defence with aid of counsel, and for the purposes hereof the Common Council shall have power to issue subpœnas, to compel the attendance of witnesses and the production of papers, when necessary, and shall proceed within ten days after service of a copy of the charges to hear and determine upon the merits of the case. If such officer shall neglect to appear and answer to such charges, his default may be deemed good cause for removal from office. The Mayor shall have power to suspend or remove from office the Marshal, Street Commissioner, Deputy Marshal, Constables, Overseers of Highways and officers of the Police; and in case of such suspension or removal, he shall report the same, with the reasons therefor, to the Common Council. **Mayor may suspend Officers.**

Sec. 20. Any officer holding office by appointment may be removed at any time by the Common Council, without charges and a trial thereof, by a vote of the majority of the Aldermen elect, except the Controller, who may be removed for the same causes and on the same proceedings as a member of the Common Council. **Removal of Officers.**

Sec. 21. Any officer holding office by election, except the Recorder, against whom charges shall be preferred, may be suspended from office by a majority vote of all the Aldermen elected, until such charges shall be heard and determined; and any officer holding office by appointment may be suspended temporarily from office, at any time, by the like vote. **Temporary Suspension from Office.**

Sec. 22. In case of expulsion or removal from office, death, resignation or permanent disability of any officer, his office shall thereby become vacant, and may be so declared by the Common Council. **Vacancies.**

Sec. 23. Resignations of office shall be made to the Common Council in writing, and be subject to their approval and acceptance. **Resignation.**

Sec. 24. If any office of appointment shall become vacant, the Common Council may appoint a successor to serve for the unexpired portion of the official term. **Filling vacancies in appointed offices.**

Sec. 25. If a vacancy occurs in the office of Mayor or Alderman more than six months before the time for holding the next succeeding annual city election, the Common Coun- **Vacancies in office of Mayor or Alderman, how filled.**

cil shall order a special election to fill such vacancy for the residue of the official term; if it occurs within six months before the time for holding such election, the Common Council may, in its discretion, order a special election to fill such vacancy for the residue of the official term.

Vacancies in other elective offices, how filled.

SEC. 26. If a vacancy occurs in any elective office, other than that of Mayor, Recorder or Alderman, the Common Council shall appoint some person eligible under this act, to serve in such office until the next annual election, when the vacancy shall be filled for the residue of the official term.

Official Bonds

SEC. 27. The Controller, Treasurer, Clerk, Attorney, Collectors, Marshal, Clerk of the Markets, Street Commissioner and Constables shall, *respectively*, before they enter upon the duties of their respective offices, and such other officers as the Common Council may direct, file in the Clerk's office an official bond, in such sum and with such sureties as the Common Council shall direct and approve.

Condition of Official Bonds

SEC. 28. The official bond of every officer shall be conditioned that he will faithfully perform the duties of his office, and will, on demand, deliver over to his successor in office, or other proper officer or agent of the corporation, all books, papers, moneys, effects and property belonging to the corporation or appertaining to his office, which may be in his custody as an officer; and such bond may be further conditioned as the Common Council shall prescribe. The official bond of every officer whose duty it may be to receive or pay out money, besides being conditioned as above required, shall be further conditioned that he will, on demand, pay over or account for to the corporation, or any proper officer or agent thereof, all moneys received by him as such officer.

Constables' Bonds.

SEC. 29. Every person elected to the office of Constable in said city, before entering on the duties of his office, shall, with two or more sureties, to be approved by the Common Council, execute and file with the City Clerk a bond to the City of Detroit in the penal sum of two thousand dollars, or an instrument in writing, conditioned well and faithfully in all things, to execute and perform the duties of his office during the continuance therein, and to pay to each and every person who may be entitled thereto, all sums of money which said Constable may become liable to pay on account of any execution or process for the collection of money which shall be delivered to him; and further conditioned as the Common Council may prescribe. Condition.

SEC. 30. The Common Council may at any time require any officer, whether elected or appointed, to execute and file with the Clerk of the City new official bonds in the same or in such further sums, and with new or such further sureties, as said Council may deem requisite for the interest of the corporation. Renewal of Official Bonds

SEC. 31. The Clerk of the City shall cause every officer, whether elected or appointed, as soon as practicable after his election or appointment, to be served with a written notice thereof and of the amount of his official bond; and if such officer shall neglect to take and subscribe his oath of office, or to file his required official bond within the time prescribed therefor by this act; or if any officer, required to execute and file a new official bond, as provided in the preceding section, shall not comply with such requirement within ten days after notice thereof from the City Clerk, the Common Council may declare the office in such case vacant, and such vacancy may be filled as heretofore provided in this act. Notice of Election to Office. Neglect to qualify.

SEC. 32. The Common Council, or such officer as the Common Council shall by resolution or ordinance prescribe, may examine into the sufficiency of the proposed sureties in any official bond or instrument in writing required by this act, or in any contract in writing, to which the corporation or any officer or board under this act shall be a party in interest, and may require such sureties to submit to an examination under oath as to their property and responsibility. The depositions of the surety shall be reduced to writing, be signed by him, certified by the person taking the same, and annexed to and filed with the bond or instrument in writing to which it relates. Sureties in Official Bonds may be required to justify on Oath.

City Clerk to report delinquents to Council.

SEC. 33. The Clerk of the City shall report the name of any person elected or appointed to any office, who shall have neglected to file his official bond and oath of office, as required by this act, to the Common Council at its next meeting after such default.

CHAPTER III.

ELECTIONS—HOW CONDUCTED.

Annual City election, time, place and notice.

SECTION 1. The annual city election shall be held on the first Tuesday after the first Monday of November in each year, at such places in the several wards as shall be designated by an order of the Common Council, at least twenty days previous thereto, notice of which, specifying, also, the officers to be elected and the time for opening and closing the polls, shall immediately, or within three days after the date of such order, be given by the City Clerk by publication in two or more daily newspapers published in said city. The time and place for holding a special election shall be designated, and the notice thereof given in the same manner and to the same effect.

Special elections.

Election Districts.

SEC. 2. Each ward shall be an election district; every elector shall vote in the ward in which he resides, and the residence of an elector under this act shall be the ward in which he takes his regular meals.

Inspectors of election.

SEC. 3. At every election, the inspectors of election for the ward in which such election may be held, shall consist of the two Aldermen of the ward, and a third person to be chosen, *viva voce*, by the electors present, from their number, at the time of opening the polls, and if from any cause either or both of said Aldermen shall fail to attend any such election, his or their places may be supplied for the purpose of such election by the electors present, who shall elect any of their number, *viva voce*. Said inspectors, before entering upon their duties, shall each take the same oath of office prescribed for other officers under this act.

Oath of Inspectors.

SEC. 4. The inspectors in each ward, before the opening of the polls, shall appoint two competent clerks of the election, who shall take the same oath as the inspectors, which oath either of the inspectors may administer. Clerks of Election.

SEC. 5. One suitable ballot box, with lock and key, shall be provided and kept by the City Clerk, at the expense of the city, for each ward; and it shall be the duty of the City Clerk to deposit such box, with the key, in the hands of the inspectors for each ward, prior to the opening of the polls. Ballot Box.

SEC. 6. The polls of election shall be opened at eight o'clock in the forenoon, or as soon thereafter as may be, on the day of election, and shall be continued open until five o'clock in the afternoon of the same day, and no longer. Opening and closing polls.

SEC. 7. The qualifications of electors under this act shall be those prescribed in the first section of the seventh article of the constitution of this State, which is as follows: "In all elections every white male citizen, every white male inhabitant residing in the State on the twenty-fourth day of June one thousand eight hundred and thirty five; every white male inhabitant residing in this State on the first day of January, one thousand eight hundred and fifty, who has declared his intention to become a citizen of the United States, pursuant to the laws thereof, six months preceding an election, or who has resided in this State two years and six months and declared his intention as aforesaid, and every civilized male inhabitant of Indian descent, a native of the United States, and not a member of any tribe, shall be an elector and entitled to vote; but no citizen or inhabitant shall be an elector or entitled to vote at any election, unless he shall be above the age of twenty-one years, and has resided in this State three months, and in the township or ward in which he offers to vote, ten days next preceding such election." Qualification of voters.

SEC. 8. If at any election a vote shall be challenged, either of the inspectors of election shall be authorized to swear or affirm the person whose vote is challenged, to answer such questions as may be put to him touching his qualifications Challenge and oath.

as an elector, and said inspectors shall decide from such examination as to the legality of such vote.

Perjury. Punishment.

SEC. 9. If any person thus sworn or affirmed shall willfully swear or affirm falsely, as to any material matter concerning his qualifications as an elector of said city, he shall be deemed guilty of perjury, and may be prosecuted therefor, and, on conviction thereof, be punished by a fine not exceeding one thousand dollars, or imprisonment at hard labor in the State Prison for a period not exceeding five years, or both, at the discretion of the Court.

Punishment for voting more than once.

SEC. 10. If any person shall vote in more than one ward, or more than once in the same ward, at any election in said city, he may be prosecuted therefor, and, on conviction, shall be punished by a fine not exceeding five hundred dollars, or imprisonment at hard labor in the State Prison for a period not exceeding three years, or both, in the discretion of the Court.

Conducting Elections.

SEC. 11. The manner of conducting and voting at elections to be held under this act, the keeping of the poll lists, canvassing of the votes, certifying the returns, and all other proceedings connected with such elections, shall be the same, as nearly as may be, as is now or may hereafter be provided for by the laws of this State, applicable to general State elections, except as may be otherwise provided in this act.

Certifying returns of election. Canvass.

SEC. 12. On canvassing the votes, the inspectors shall certify a full and true return thereof, under their hands, to the Clerk of the City, carefully sealed up, together with the poll lists and ballots, within forty-eight hours after the closing of the polls; and the inspectors of election, or a majority of them, shall, on the Saturday next after election, at three o'clock in the afternoon, meet at the City Clerk's office or Common Council room, and proceed to open and canvass the said returns, and declare the result of the election.

Conducting special elections.

SEC. 13. Special elections shall be conducted, as near as may be, in the same manner as general elections, but in such cases the returns of the inspectors shall be opened and canvassed, and the result declared by the Common Council at its first meeting after the making of said returns.

SEC. 14. If any person be voted for at any election, to fill a vacancy or residue of a term, the ballots of the electors shall designate such vacancy or residue. Ballots for vacancy. To designate vacancy.

SEC. 15. In the canvass of votes, any person who has received a plurality of the votes for any office, shall be declared duly elected to such office. Plurality to elect.

SEC. 16. When two or more persons shall have an equal number of votes for the same office, the election shall be determined by the drawing of lots in the presence of the Common Council. The names of each of such persons shall be written on separate slips of paper and deposited in a box or other proper place, and the President of the Common Council shall draw out of said box or other place, in the usual manner of determining by lot, one of said slips, and the person whose name is thereon, shall be deemed entitled to hold the office for which he received said votes, in the same manner as other officers duly elected. Proceedings in case of tie.

SEC. 17. The mode of conducting all State, District and County elections in said city shall be in the manner herein provided for the election of city officers, except that the returns thereof shall be made to the County Clerk, and the same proceedings had, as near as may be, as are now or may hereafter be provided by law for the return of votes by township inspectors of election. Mode of conducti'g State, District and County elections.

SEC. 18. No person entitled to vote at any election held under this act, shall be arrested on civil process within said city, on the day on which such election is held. Privilege from arrest.

SEC. 19. The first election under this act shall be held on the first Tuesday after the first Monday in November, 1857, and all officers now holding office, by election in said city, which are made elective by the people under this act, shall continue to hold their respective offices until the second Tuesday in January, 1858. The Aldermen of said city who were elected in the year 1855, shall continue in office until the First election time of.

3

Officers holding office to continue.

second Tuesday in January, 1858, and shall be succeeded in office by the Aldermen who are elected in November, 1857, and the Aldermen who were elected in the year 1856, shall continue in office until the second Tuesday in January, 1859, and shall be succeeded in office by the Aldermen who are elected in November, 1858. In all cases where any new office is created, or where any vacancy may occur, under the provisions of this act, the Common Council may appoint persons to fill the same until the second Tuesday in January, 1858, when their successors shall be appointed, except the Assessor, who shall be appointed for his full term, as herein provided. The present Recorder of said city shall continue to hold his office until the second Tuesday in January, 1858, and shall possess and exercise the powers and duties now possessed and exercised by him under the present charter of said city; and shall also be President of the Common Council, and shall possess and exercise the powers and duties of that office, as herein provided, until the expiration of his term of office, and shall receive such salary as the Common Council may prescribe. The present Controller of said city shall continue to hold his office until the first day of April, 1859. The office of Ward Assessor is hereby abolished.

CHAPTER IV.

OFFICERS—THEIR RIGHTS, POWERS AND DUTIES.

Mayor, his duty.

SECTION 1. The Mayor shall be the chief executive officer of the City of Detroit, and conservator of its peace. It shall be his duty to keep an office in some convenient place in said city, to be provided by the Common Council; to see that all officers of said city faithfully comply with and discharge their official duties; to see that all laws pertaining to the municipal government of said city, and all ordinances and resolutions of the Common Council be faithfully observed and executed;

and he shall have power, in his discretion, to report to the Common Council any violations thereof. He shall, from time to time, give to the Common Council such information and recommend such measures as he shall deem necessary or expedient.

Salary of Mayor.

SEC. 2. The Mayor shall be paid a salary of twelve hundred dollars. In case of a vacancy in the office of Mayor, or of his being unable to perform the duties of his office, by reason of sickness, absence from the city or other cause, the President of the Common Council shall be acting Mayor; and in case at the same time there shall also be a vacancy in the office of President of the Common Council, or he shall be unable to perform the duties of his office, by reason of sickness, absence from the city or other cause, the President *pro tempore* of the Common Council shall be acting Mayor; and such acting Mayor shall be vested with all the powers, and shall perform all the duties of Mayor, until the vacancy or vacancies aforesaid be filled, or the Mayor or President of the Common Council, as the case may be, shall resume his office.

Who is to be acting Mayor in certain cases.

President of Com. Council

SEC. 3. The Common Council shall, at its first meeting in January in each year, select from their number a President for the year, and in case of a vacancy or his temporary absence, supply his place by the election of a President *pro tempore.*

In certain cases Presid't *pro tempore* to preside.

SEC. 4. The President *pro tempore* of the Common Council shall preside at its meetings, in case of a vacancy in the office of President of the Common Council, or of his being unable from any cause to be present and preside. In such case the President *pro tempore* shall be invested with all the power, and shall perform all the duties, of President of the Common Council, until he shall resume his office, or the vacancy therein be filled.

Powers of

Duties of Attorney.

SEC. 5. The Attorney shall appear in and conduct all suits, prosecutions and proceedings in the Recorder's Court, to which the City of Detroit is a party, to the end thereof, subject to the rules and practice of said court, and if the same be removed to any other tribunal by writ of error, habeas corpus or otherwise, he shall conduct the case before such tribunal.

Duties of Clerk.

SEC. 6. The Clerk of the corporation shall keep the corporate seal and all papers filed in or pertaining to his office, and shall be Clerk of the Common Council, shall attend its meetings, and shall make and preserve a record of all its ordinances, resolutions and other proceedings in proper books to be provided therefor, and when requested, shall duly certify, under the corporate seal, copies thereof, and of all papers duly filed in his office pertaining to the same, and shall possess and exercise the powers of Township Clerks.

Duties of Controller.

SEC. 7. It shall be the duty of the Controller to countersign all bonds which the corporation or Common Council is authorized to issue, pledging the faith and credit of said city; to receive all accounts and demands against the corporation, examine them in detail, audit and allow them, or such parts thereof as to the correctness of which he has no doubt, and which the claimant is willing to accept in full discharge thereof, file and number them as vouchers, in the order of their allowance, register them with the amount allowed and date of allowance in the same order in a proper book, provided for such purpose, and, on their being properly discharged in writing, to draw and sign his warrant therefor upon the Treasurer, when the same is ordered to be paid by the Common Council. If he shall have any doubt concerning their correctness, he shall register them in a separate list and return them to the Common Council with his objections. If the same be allowed by the Common Council, in pursuance of their authority under this act, on their return to the Controller, with a certificate of the Clerk endorsed thereon that they have been allowed by the Common Council, he shall then file and register them in the list of allowed claims, in the same manner as above provided for the registering of claims audited and allowed by him, and, on their being

File vouchers

Draw Warrants.

Register doubtful accounts and return to Common Council.

properly discharged in writing, shall draw and sign his warrant therefor on the Treasurer. It shall also be the duty of the Controller to lay before the Common Council once in each year, in the month of April, or oftener if directed by the Common Council, a schedule of all accounts audited and allowed by him, and of all leases of the property of the corporation, specifying the name of the lessees, the rates of rent, and the period when the leases will terminate. It shall also be the duty of the Controller to examine the tax rolls and returns of the city officers, and take general supervision of the financial concerns of the corporation; to keep a complete set of books exhibiting the financial condition of the corporation in its various departments and funds, its resources and liabilities, with a proper classification thereof, and each fund or appropriation for any distinct object of expenditure or class of expenditures. When any such fund or appropriation has been exhausted by warrants already drawn thereon, or by appropriations, liabilities, debts and expenses actually made, incurred or contracted for, and to be paid out of such fund or appropriation, the Controller shall advise the Common Council thereof at its next meeting.

To present to Council schedule of accounts, &c.

To examine tax rolls and returns of City Officers.

To advise Common Council when any fund is exhausted.

SEC. 8. The Controller shall also open an account with the Treasurer, in which he shall charge said Treasurer with the whole amount of taxes, general and special, levied in said city, also the whole amount in detail of all bonds, notes, mortgages, leases, rents, interest and other moneys receivable, in order that the value and description of all personal property belonging to the corporation may at any time be known. He shall also keep a list of all the property, real, personal and mixed, belonging to the corporation, and of all its debts and liabilities, in order that the amount of the moneys and liabilities of the corporation may at any time be known at his office. The Controller shall also perform such other duties as are prescribed by this act, or may be prescribed by the Common Council, subject to the provisions hereof. The Controller shall also open accounts with the Treasurer, in which

To open an account with Treasurer.

To keep a list of property of corporation.

he shall charge him with all moneys appropriated, raised or received for each of the several funds of the corporation, and credit him for all warrants drawn thereon, keeping a separate account of debit and credit for each fund, charging every warrant drawn to the account of the particular fund constituted or raised for the specific purpose for which such warrant is drawn, in order that it may be known at the Controller's office when each fund has been or may be exhausted, and what balance, if any, may remain therein.

SEC. 9. The Recorder and the Clerk of the Recorder's Court shall possess and exercise the powers and duties elsewhere prescribed in this act.

Duties of Treasurer.

SEC. 10. The Treasurer shall have the custody of all moneys, bonds, mortgages, notes, leases and evidences of value belonging to the corporation. He shall receive all moneys belonging to and receivable by the corporation, and keep an accurate account of all receipts and expenditures thereof. He shall pay no money out of the treasury, except in pursuance of and by authority of law, and on a warrant signed by the Controller, which shall specify the purpose for which the amount thereof is to be paid. He shall keep an accurate account of and be charged with all taxes and moneys appropriated, raised or received for each fund of the corporation; shall keep a separate account for each fund, and shall pay every warrant out of the particular fund constituted or raised for the purposes for which said warrant was issued, and having the name of such fund endorsed thereon by the Controller. He shall exhibit to the Common Council annually, and as often and for such period as may be required, a full and detailed account of all receipts and disbursements since the date of his last annual report, classifying them by the fund to which such receipts are credited, and out of which such disbursements are made; shall report to the Controller, at the end of each month, the amount received and credited by him to each fund, and on what account received; and shall also, when required, exhibit a general statement showing the financial condition of the treasury, which account, report and statement shall be filed in the office of the Controller.

SEC. 11. The Marshal shall possess and exercise the powers and duties, as a conservator of the peace, which Township Constables under the general laws of this State possess and may exercise, and shall possess and exercise such other powers and duties as shall be prescribed by the Common Council for the preservation of the public peace, and shall possess and exercise the same powers for the service and execution of all writs, process and warrants issuing out of the Recorder's Court, in cases arising under the ordinances of the city, which Sheriffs now have or may have by law for the service and execution of writs and process issuing from the Circuit Courts of this State. He shall obey and execute all lawful precepts and commands of said Common Council and of said Recorder's Court; shall attend the sittings of said court, and he, or one of his deputies, shall attend the meetings of said Common Council.

Powers and duties of Marshal.

SEC. 12. Assistant Marshals shall have and exercise the same powers and duties as the Marshal.

Assistant Marshals.

SEC. 13. The Surveyor shall have power, and it shall be his duty, to survey within the corporation limits. He shall have the same power to make surveys and plats within the corporation limits as are now or may hereafter be given by law to County Surveyors, and the like effect and validity shall be given to his official acts, surveys and plats, as are or may hereafter be given by law to the official acts, surveys and plats of County Surveyors. He shall make out the assessment rolls for paving, for side and crosswalks, for lateral sewers, and for all other special assessments, and shall survey for the city.

Surveyor's powers and duties.

SEC. 14. It shall be the duty of the Collector of the corporation to collect assessments for constructing or paving sidewalks and crosswalks, for paving streets and alleys, and such special assessments as may be imposed and levied by the Common Council.

Collector's duties.

Assessor's duties.

SEC. 15. The Assessor shall assess all the property liable to assessment, for the purpose of levying the taxes lawfully imposed thereon, as hereinafter more particularly provided. The Assessor shall also prepare and return a list of persons to serve as jurors, as hereinafter provided in this act.

Street Commissioner's duties.

SEC. 16. The Street Commissioner shall superintend the construction of pavements, repair and cleaning of sidewalks, crosswalks, streets, lanes, alleys, public places, culverts and bridges within said city.

Overseers of Highways of Wards.

SEC. 17. The Overseer of Highways for each ward shall, under the superintendence and control of the Street Commissioner, work and improve the highways, streets, lanes, alleys and public places of said city, in the ward for which he is elected, and render a true account of the expenses thereof, under oath, to the Controller.

Ward Collectors, duties of

SEC. 18. The Collector for each ward shall collect all city, highway, sewer and school taxes, and all State and county taxes assessed and imposed upon the real and personal property for such ward, and account for and pay over the same, as required by law or by ordinance, or resolution of the Common Council, which have not been paid into the City Treasury.

Director of the Poor and Constables.

SEC. 19. The Director of the Poor and Constables shall have the power and perform the duties of township officers, elected under the general laws of the State, subject to the provisions of this act.

Books, &c., to be delivered to successors in office.

SEC. 20. Whenever any officer shall resign or be removed from office, or the term for which he shall have been elected or appointed shall expire, he shall, on demand, deliver over to his successor in office all the books, papers, moneys and effects in his custody as such officer, and in any way appertaining to his office, and every person violating this provision shall be deemed guilty of a misdemeanor, and may be proceeded against in the same manner as public officers generally for the like offence, under the general laws of this State now or hereafter in force and applicable thereto, and every officer

Penalties for violation.

appointed or elected under this act shall be deemed an officer within the meaning and provisions of such general laws of the State.

SEC. 21. In addition to the rights, powers, duties and liabilities of officers prescribed in this act, all officers, whether elected or appointed, shall have such other rights, powers, duties and liabilities, subject to and consistent with the provisions of this act, as the Common Council may deem expedient and shall prescribe by ordinance or resolution. General powers and duties of officers.

SEC. 22. The Mayor, Recorder and members of the Common Council, Clerk, Controller and Clerk of the Recorder's Court are hereby authorized generally to administer oaths and to take affidavits; but neither of said officers shall receive any fees therefor, except said clerks. The Controller shall have the power to take acknowledgments of deeds under the laws of this State. Who may administer oath. Controller may take acknowledgm't of deeds.

CHAPTER V.

COMMON COUNCIL—POWERS AND DUTIES.

SECTION 1. The Aldermen of the City shall constitute the Common Council thereof, and a majority of all the Aldermen elected shall be a quorum for the transaction of business, but a smaller number may adjourn from day to day. Who constitute the Common Council.

SEC. 2. The Clerk of the City shall be Clerk of the Common Council. City Clerk to be clerk of

SEC. 3. The Common Council, at its first meeting after the annual city election, and after the newly elected Aldermen, or a majority thereof, shall have entered into their offices, shall appoint, by ballot, one of their number President, who shall serve until the first meeting of the Common Council after the next annual election, and until his successor be appointed, and shall have the powers and duties prescribed in this act. Council to appoint President.

4

Sessions of Council.

SEC. 4. The Common Council shall hold regular sessions at such times and places as they shall, by ordinance or resolution, direct, and may adjourn regular sessions from time to time, as may be deemed expedient.

Special meetings, by whom called.

SEC. 5. Special meetings of the Common Council may be called at any time by the Mayor; or if one third of all the Aldermen elected shall, in writing, request the President of the Common Council to call a special meeting, stating therein the time and objects thereof, and he shall refuse or neglect for twenty-four hours to call such meeting, a copy of such request to the President may be filed with the Clerk of the City, with the certificate of any Alderman endorsed thereon, showing the presentation thereof to the President and his refusal or neglect as aforesaid, and thereupon such special meeting shall be held, and the Clerk of the City shall cause notice thereof and of its time and place to be served on each of the members of the Common Council personally, or by leaving the same at their usual place of abode, and the proceedings of said meeting shall be limited to the objects thereof, as set forth in such request to the President. Special meetings may be adjourned from time to time, as may be deemed necessary, in order to dispose of the business which they are called to consider.

Notice of special meetings.

May be adjourned.

Ordinances and resolutions to be presented to Mayor for approval.

SEC. 6. Every ordinance, resolution or proceeding of the Common Council, imposing taxes or assessments, or originating the expenditure or disposal of money or property, or whereby the corporation or any board of officers under this act may incur any debt or liability, and every ordinance and resolution, except resolutions making appointments to or removal from office, and except ordinances and resolutions for the fixing of salaries and for the payment of debts and liabilities, previously and lawfully contracted, shall, before it takes effect, be presented by the Clerk to the Mayor. If the Mayor approve thereof, he shall thereon write his approval with the date thereof, and sign the same, and thereupon such ordinance, resolution or proceeding shall go into

If Mayor approves, he shall write and sign his approval.

effect; and such as he shall not so approve and sign, he shall return to the Common Council, with his objections thereto in writing, under cover sealed and addressed to said Common Council. If Mayor shall not approve, he shall return with his objections.

SEC. 7. If the Mayor shall neglect to approve, as aforesaid, any ordinance, resolution or proceeding, or return the same, as aforesaid, to said Common Council with his objections, at its next regular meeting after the same shall have been presented to him by the Clerk, as before provided, the same shall go into effect. Mayor's veto

SEC. 8. Upon the return, as aforesaid, of any ordinance, resolution or proceeding, the Common Council shall proceed to reconsider the vote by which the same was passed and adopted; and if, after such reconsideration, two-thirds of all the members elected shall agree by ayes and noes, which shall be entered of record, to pass or adopt the same, it shall go into effect. Reconsideration of veto'd resolutions, &c.

SEC. 9. The Clerk of the City shall, at the time of presenting any ordinance, resolution or proceeding of the Common Council to the Mayor for his approval or disapproval, make a certificate, to be endorsed thereon or attached thereto, in which he shall specify the day on which the same was so presented; and such certificate shall be recorded with the proceedings of the Common Council. Clerk's certificate of presentation. Recording certificate.

SEC. 10. All ordinances, resolutions and written proceedings of the Common Council shall be deposited in the office of the Clerk of the City, who shall safely keep the same; and they shall be recorded in proper books, to be provided therefor. He shall keep a journal record of the proceedings of the Common Council, and also a record of every ordinance enacted and of the time of its first publication, which record shall be signed by the Clerk and by the President of the Common Council. Ordinances, &c., deposit'd with clerk and recorded. Clerk to keep journal and record.

SEC. 11. All proceedings of the Common Council shall be published in some daily newspaper published in said city. All ordinances shall be published for six successive days in Publication of proceedings.

the official daily newspaper of said city, and in one other daily newspaper published in said city, and shall take effect in ten days after their enactment: *Provided, however*, That the Common Council may fix and prescribe therein a different period, and that no ordinance shall take effect before at least one publication thereof.

Proviso.

Style of ordinances.

SEC. 12. The style of ordinances shall be: "It is hereby ordained by the Common Council of the City of Detroit."

Council meetings to be public.

SEC. 13. All meetings of the Common Council shall be public, and its proceedings and records shall be open to public inspection at reasonable times.

Right of Petition.

SEC. 14. The inhabitants of said city shall have the right to petition the Common Council.

Council to be judge of qualification of its members.

SEC. 15. The Common Council shall be the judge of the election and qualifications of its own members, and shall have the power to determine contested elections, to compel the attendance of absent members, to determine the rules of its proceedings, and pass all by-laws and rules necessary and convenient for the transaction of business, and not inconsistent with the provisions of this act.

Council's powers over city property

SEC. 16. The Common Council shall have the general management and control of the finances and all the property, real, personal and mixed, belonging to the corporation, whether lying within or beyond the limits of said city, with full power to lease, sell, convey, transfer and dispose of the same absolutely; and shall have power to make all necessary regulations for preserving and protecting the same from destruction, decay or injury, and concerning the management thereof.

Money resolution, &c., not to be passed at same meeting at which it is introduced.

SEC. 17. No resolution, ordinance or proceeding of the Common Council, imposing taxes or assessments, or requiring the payment, expenditure or disposal of money or property, or creating a debt or liability therefor, and no other ordinance shall be passed at the same meeting at which it was introduced, unless by unanimous consent, or at a special meeting called therefor; and every such ordinance, resolution or pro-

Exception.

ceeding shall be passed by yeas and nays, to be entered on the record; and, upon the demand of one-fourth of the members present, the yeas and nays shall be taken on any question and entered on the record. Yeas and Nays.

SEC. 18. No Alderman shall vote on any question in which he is interested; on all other questions every Alderman present shall vote, and in all cases of a tie vote the question shall be lost. Aldermen interested not to vote.

SEC. 19. All appointments to office shall be made by a majority vote of all the Aldermen elected, and removals from office shall be made by the like vote, except in cases where by this act a different vote may be required. Appointments and removals by majority vote.

SEC. 20. The President of the Common Council shall appoint such committees as the Common Council may deem necessary. The duties of standing committees shall be prescribed by general ordinance. Standing Committees.

SEC. 21. The chairman of any committee, and the members of any board established by or under this act, may administer oaths and take affidavits in respect to any matter pending before such committee or board; such committees or board shall have power to subpœna witnesses, to compel their attendance, and the production of necessary papers in all examinations pending before them, and to that end the Common Council may prescribe and regulate the necessary proceedings, and confer upon the Marshal or other officer of the corporation all needful powers for the purposes aforesaid. Powers of Chairman of Committees.

SEC. 22. The Common Council, in addition to its other powers under this act, and subject to and consistently with its provisions, shall have power within the limits and jurisdiction of the corporation: Powers of Council.

1st. To determine and regulate the compensation of all officers elected or appointed under this act, except as is herein otherwise provided; but the compensation of no officer, fixed by an annual or periodical salary, shall be diminished during the term for which he was elected or appointed. The salary Compensation of officers. Salary.

of no officer shall be increased during his term of office, unless by a two-thirds vote of the Common Council.

Appointments and removals. 2d. To provide for and regulate the election and appointment of all officers, and for their removal from office, and for the filling of vacancies, subject to this act.

Fees and costs. 3d. To authorize and regulate the demand and receipt, by officers, of such fees and costs, and in such cases as the Common Council may deem reasonable.

Fees of jurors and witnesses 4th. To fix and regulate the fees of jurors and witnesses in any proceeding under this act, or under any ordinance of the Common Council.

River Detroit 5th. To provide for and preserve the purity and salubrity of the waters of the Detroit River; to prohibit and prevent the depositing therein of all filthy and other matter tending to render said water impure, unwholesome or offensive; to preserve and regulate the navigation of the said river within the limits of said city; to prohibit and prevent the depositing or keeping therein any structure, earth or substance tending to obstruct or impair the navigation thereof, and remove all obstructions that may, at any time, occur therein, and to direct and regulate the stationing, anchoring and mooring of vessels, and laying out of cargoes and ballast from the same.

Ferries. 6th. To license, continue and regulate so many ferries from within said city to the opposite shore of the Detroit River, for carrying and transporting persons and property across said river, in such manner as shall seem most conducive to the public good.

Wharves and docks. 7th. To erect, repair and regulate public wharves and docks at the ends of streets and on the property of the corporation; to regulate the erection and repair of private wharves and docks, so that they shall not extend into the Detroit River beyond a certain line, to be established by the Common Council; and to prohibit the encumbering of all public wharves and docks with boxes, carriages, carts, drays, sleighs, sleds or other vehicle or thing whatsoever.

8th. To lease the wharves and wharfing privileges at the ends of streets on the Detroit River in said city, upon such terms and conditions, and under such covenants, and with such remedies in case of non-performance as the Common Council may direct; but no buildings shall be erected thereon. No lease thereof shall be executed for a longer period than three years, and a free passage at all times for all persons with their baggage over said public wharves. **Leases of wharves.**

9th. To work and improve all highways, avenues, streets, lanes, alleys and public spaces within said city; to assess and levy upon all taxable property within said city, and expend such highway taxes as may be necessary therefor, and to elect whether the same shall be collected in money or labor, in such amount as the Common Council shall prescribe for each ward respectively: *Provided*, such highway taxes shall not in amount exceed the rates now fixed by law, and the same shall be collected, assessed and levied as other taxes. **Highways and streets.** **Proviso.**

10th. To make, grade, improve and adorn the public parks, squares, spaces, and all grounds in said city belonging to or under the control of the corporation, and to control and regulate the same consistently with the purposes and objects thereof. **Public parks, &c.**

11th. To establish, open, widen, extend, straighten, alter, vacate and abolish highways, streets, avenues, lanes, alleys and public grounds or spaces within said city, and to grade, pave, repair and otherwise improve the highways, streets, avenues, lanes, alleys or interior public spaces, created by the intersection of streets, crosswalks and sidewalks in said city with stone, wood, brick or other material; and the Common Council shall have full power and authority to provide for paying the costs and expenses thereof by assessment on the owner of the lot or premises in front of or adjacent to which such highways, streets, avenues, lanes, alleys, interior or public spaces, crosswalks or sidewalks may be directed to be graded, paved, re-paved or otherwise improved: *Provided*, that the cost of such grading, paving, repairing or improving **Opening streets, &c.** **Paving costs and expenses** **Proviso.**

such interior or public spaces shall be assessed to each block, in such proportion as the Common Council shall deem just and equitable; *Provided further*, that each block shall only be assessed to the centre of such interior or public spaces each way, which assessment shall be a lien, until paid, on such lot or premises in front of or adjacent to which such grading, paving, repairing and improving may be directed, and shall be collected in the same manner as other assessments or taxes imposed by authority of the Common Council. Whenever such grading, paving, repairing and improving shall be at the intersection of two or more avenues or streets, and in front of or adjacent to the point of a triangular block, such portion of the costs and expenses thereof shall be assessed to and paid by the City of Detroit, as the Common Council shall deem just.

2d Proviso.

Dirt, &c.

12th. To sell or otherwise provide for disposing of all dirt, filth, manure and cleanings lying in or gathered from highways, streets, avenues, lanes, alleys and public spaces, and all earth to be removed therefrom or from the public squares and grounds of said city, in grading, paving or otherwise improving the same.

Cleaning streets, &c.

13th. To clean the highways, streets, avenues, lanes, alleys, public grounds and squares, crosswalks and sidewalks in said city of filth, mud and other substances; to prohibit and prevent the incumbering thereof with boxes, signs, posts and all other materials or things whatsoever, and to remove the same therefrom; to prevent the exhibition of signs on canvass or otherwise in and upon any vehicle standing or traveling upon the streets of said city; to control, prescribe and regulate the mode of constructing and suspending awnings, and the exhibition and suspension of signs therein; to compel the occupants of lots to clean the sidewalks in front of and adjacent thereto of snow, ice, dirt, mud, boxes and every incumbrance or obstruction thereon; to control, prescribe and regulate the manner in which the highways, streets, avenues, lanes, alleys, public grounds and spaces within said city shall be used and enjoyed; to direct and regulate the planting and provide for the preservation of ornamental trees therein; to provide for and regulate the lighting of the same, and the erection of lamps and lamp posts therein; to prohibit and prevent racing and fast or dangerous driving and riding therein; to prohibit and prevent the flying of kites, and all practices, amusements and doings therein having a tendency to frighten teams and horses, or dangerous to life or property; to remove or caused to be removed all walls and other structures that may be liable to fall therein, or otherwise, so as to endanger life or property.

14th. To prohibit and prevent any riot, rout, disorderly noise, disturbance or assemblage, or the crying of any goods in the streets or elsewhere in said city. **Riots, &c.**

15th. To preserve quiet and order on the docks and in the streets of said city, at the arrival and departure of rail road cars, steamboats and other vessels, and prescribe and regulate the manner and places in which drivers, porters, runners, solicitors, agents and baggage collectors for hotels or public houses or express companies, draymen, cabmen, cartmen, hackmen, omnibus drivers and solicitors for passengers or for baggage with their drays, carts, cabs, carriages, sleighs or other vehicles shall stand, and to prohibit or prevent them from entering or driving within any rail road depot, or upon any wharf or dock, or entering upon any steamboat or other vessel, to solicit passengers or for baggage. **Quiet on docks and streets.**

16th. To prescribe places or stands in the streets of said city, within which drays, carts, cabs, hacks, coaches, carriages, sleighs, sleds and other vehicles may stand and be kept for hire, and within which loads of wood, coal, hay and other articles may be kept for sale, and to regulate such stands and places. **Stands for vehicles.**

17th. To prohibit and prevent the exhibition of fire-works and firing of cannon or any fire-arms, which the Common Couucil may deem dangerous to life or property. **Fire-works.**

18th. To permit any person to pave or plank the side-walks in front of the premises owned or occupied by such person **Paving side-walks.**

5

in said city, under the direction of the Street Commissioners or some other officer of the corporation, and according to such regulations as the Comon Council shall prescribe; and whenever any street shall have been paved, gravelled, planked or macadamised by the Common Council, and the assessment for the costs and expenses thereof has been duly paid to the corporation, such person shall not be assessed or compelled to pay any district, road or highway tax on the premises in front of which such pavement shall have been made, so long as he shall keep the same in repair, to the satisfaction of the Common Council.

Indecent exposure of person, &c.

19th. To prohibit and prevent, in the streets or elsewhere in said city, indecent exposure of the person, the show, sale or exhibition for sale of indecent or obscene pictures, drawings, engravings, paintings and books or pamphlets, and all indecent or obscene exhibitions and shows of every kind.

Cattle at large in streets.

20th. To prohibit and prevent or regulate the leading and driving or running at large of cattle, horses, asses, mules, swine, sheep, goats, geese and domestic fowls in the streets or elsewhere in said city, and to impound the same, when running at large, in one or more sufficient pounds, to be provided and maintained by the city, and to sell the same to pay the costs of proceedings and any penalty thereby incurred, rendering the surplus, if any, to the owner.

Dogs.

21st. To prohibit and prevent or regulate the running at large of dogs, to require them to be muzzled, and to authorize their destruction, when running at large in violation of any ordinance of the Common Council; to compel persons to fasten or secure their horses, oxen or other animals attached to vehicles or otherwise, while standing or remaining in the streets, lanes or alleys of said city; to prohibit and prevent persons from driving or riding in vehicles or otherwise upon or across the side-walks of said city.

Securing teams. **Driving on side-walks.**

Bridges, culverts, sewers and drains.

22d. To establish, construct, maintain, repair, enlarge and discontinue within the highways, streets, avenues, lanes, alleys and public spaces of said city such bridges, culverts sewers, drains and lateral drains and sewers, as the Common Council may see fit, with a view to the proper sewerage and drainage of said city; to compel the owners of all occupied lots, premises, and subdivisions thereof within said city, to construct private drains or sewers therefrom, to connect with some public sewer or drain. Said private drains and sewers shall be constructed in such manner and of such form and dimensions, and under such regulations as the Common Council shall prescribe.

23d. To assess, levy and collect an annual assessment or tax on all lots and subdivisions thereof, and on all cellars drained by private drains or sewers connected with any public sewer or drain, as hereafter further provided. **Assessment on cellars, lots, &c.**

24th. To survey, ascertain and establish the boundaries of the city and of all highways, streets, avenues, lanes, alleys, public parks, squares and spaces in said city; to prohibit and remove all encroachments upon the same by buidings, fences or in any other manner; and to number the buildings, the expense of such numbering to be assessed against and collected of the owner or occupant. **Boundaries of city and streets.** **Number buildings.**

25th. To provide for the draining of any swamp, marsh, wet or low lands in said city, or within the distance of three miles therefrom, by the opening of ditches; but a jury of not less than six disinterested freeholders of the County of Wayne, before any proposed ditch can be opened, shall ascertain that the opening thereof is necessary or proper; also, whether the benefits which will accrue to the owner or owners of any lands from the opening of the ditch, will or will not be equal to any damages, he or they will sustain thereby. If such benefits are exceeded by the damages, they shall ascertain and certify the damages to which the owner or owners will be entitled, after deducting therefrom the amount of benefits their lands will receive from the opening of the proposed ditch. On payment or tender of the damages thus ascertained and certified, the Common Council shall have power to enter **Draining Swamps.**

upon any land through which the proposed ditch will run, with the necessary agents, teams and implements, to cut and open said ditch, to protect, clean and scour it from time to time, so as to preserve its original dimensions, and to prohibit and prevent all obstruction thereof or injury thereto.

Markets. 26th. To erect and maintain market-houses, establish markets and market-places; to lease market stalls, booths and stands; to provide fully for the good government and regulations thereof, and to prohibit, prevent and punish forestalling and regrating.

Public health 27th. To provide for the preservation of the general health of the inhabitants of said city; to make regulations to secure the same; to prevent the introduction or spreading of contagious or infectious diseases; to prevent and suppress diseases generally, and, if deemed necessary, to establish a Board of Health and prescribe and regulate its powers and duties.

Abatement of nuisances. 28th. To prohibit, prevent, abate and remove all nuisances in said city, or within the distance therefrom of half a mile and to punish the authors or maintainers thereof, and authorize and direct the speedy or immediate abatement or removal of nuisances by some officer of said city. If, in order to abate or remove any nuisance, the Common Council shall deem it necessary to fill up, level or drain any lot or premises, they shall have power so to do; to assess the cost and expenses of such filling, levelling or draining, and impose the same as an assessment or tax on said lot or premises, which shall be a lien thereon till paid, and shall be collected in the same manner as other taxes and assessments levied and imposed by authority of the Common Council.

Nuisances. 29th. To compel the owner or occupant of any grocery, cellar, tallow-chandler's shop, soap, candle, starch or glue factory, tannery, butcher's shop or stall, slaughter-house, stable, barn, privy, sewer, or other unwholesome or nauseous house or place, to cleanse, remove or abate the same, whenever necessary for the health, comfort or convenience of the inhabitants of said city.

30th. To prohibit and prevent any person from burying, depositing or leaving within the limits of said city, or within one mile distant therefrom, or keeping or having on the premises owned or occupied by him in said city, any dead carcass, putrid or unsound beef, pork, fish, hides and skins and any article, substance or thing that is unwholesome or nauseous, and to compel and authorize the removal thereof by some officer of said city; or to compel any person so bringing, depositing or leaving the same within the limits of said city, or one mile distant therefrom, or having or keeping the same on the premises owned or occupied by him in said city, to remove the same. Nuisances.

31st. To direct and regulate the construction of cellars, slips, barns, private drains, sinks and privies; to compel the owner or occupant to fill up, drain, cleanse, alter, relay or repair the same, or to cause the same to be done by some officer of the corporation, and assess the expenses thereof on the lot or premises having such cellar, slip, barn, private drain, sink or privy thereon, which assessment shall be a lien on such lot or premises, and be collected in the same manner as other assessments imposed by authority of the Common Council. To direct and regulate the construction of lateral sewers or drains, for the purpose of more effectually draining all lots or cellars, yards and sinks within the limits of said city, whenever, in their opinion, the same shall be necessary: *Provided*, Such lateral sewers or drains shall be laid or constructed through any of the streets and alleys adjoining or in front of the premises through which sewers or drains shall be ordered constructed, and assess the expense thereof on such lots or premises benefitted thereby, which assessment shall be a lien on such lots or premises until paid, and be collected in the same manner as other assessments imposed by authority of the Common Council. Cellars. Proviso.

32. To establish a fire department; to provide for the pre- Fire Depart't

vention and extinguishment of fires, and to establish, organize and regulate fire companies in the manner elsewhere prescribed in this act.

Powder or other factory or buildings.

33d. To prohibit and prevent within certain limits in said city, to be determined by the Common Council, the location or construction of buildings for storing powder, powder factories, tanneries, distilleries, buildings for the manufacture of turpentine, camphene and dangerous or easily inflammable or explosive substances, slaughter-houses and yards, butchering shops, soap, candle, starch and glue factories, establishments for steaming or rendering lard, tallow, offal and such other substances, as can be rendered into tallow, lard or oil, and all establishments where any nauseous, offensive or unwholesome business may be carried on. And such buildings, factories, shops and establishments as aforesaid, now or hereafter to be constructed in said city, whether within or without the limits, to be determined as aforesaid, together with blacksmith shops, founderies, cooper shops, steam boiler factories, carpenter shops, planing establishments, breweries and all buildings and establishments usually regarded as extra-hazardous in respect to fire, shall be subject to such regulations in relation to their construction and management as the Common Council may make with a view to the protection of any property from injury by fire, or to the health and safety of the inhabitants of said city, and to prevent their becoming in any way nuisances.

Safe-guards against fire.

34th. To regulate the keeping and conveyance in said city of powder and other combustible or dangerous articles, and the use and kind of lights or lamps to be used in barns, stables, and all buildings and establishments usually regarded as extra-hazardous in respect to fire.

Wooden buildings, construction, removal and re-building.

35th. To prohibit and prevent the location or construction of any wooden or frame-house, store, shop, or other building on such streets, alleys and places, or within such limits in said city as the Common Council may from time to time prescribe; to prohibit and prevent the removing of wooden or frame buildings from any part of said city to any lot on such streets, alleys and places, or within said limits, and the rebuilding and repairing of the same; to prevent the rebuilding or repairing of wooden buildings on said streets, alleys and places, or within said limits, when damaged by fire or otherwise. May be prohibited.

36th. To regulate the construction of partition fences and of partition and parapet walls, the thickness of walls and the size of brick; to regulate the construction of chimneys, hearths, fire-places, fire-arches, ovens, and the putting up of stoves, stove-pipes, kettles, boilers, or any structure or apparatus that may be dangerous in causing or promoting fires; to prohibt and prevent the burning out of chimneys and chimney-flues; to compel and regulate the cleaning thereof, and fix the fees therefor; to compel and regulate the construction of ash-houses or deposits for ashes; to compel the owners of houses and other buildings to have scuttles upon the roofs thereof and stairs or ladders leading to the same; to appoint one or more officers to enter into all buildings and enclosures, to discover whether the same are in a dangerous state, and to cause such as are in a dangerous state to be put in a safe condition; to authorize any of the officers of the city to keep away from the vicinity of a fire all idle or suspicious persons, and to compel all officers of the city and other persons, to aid in the extinguishment of fires and in the preservation of property exposed to danger therefrom. Partition fences, walls, chimneys, &c Safe-guards against fire. Officers at fires.

37th. To prohibit and prevent or to regulate bathing and swimming in any of the waters in and adjoining said city, determine the times and places thereof, and prohibit and prevent any obscene or indecent exhibition, exposure or conduct thereat. Bathing.

38th. To prohibit, prevent and suppress the keeping of houses of ill fame or assignation, or for the resort of common prostitutes, disorderly houses and disorderly groceries; to restrain, suppress and punish the keepers thereof; to punish, restrain and prevent common prostitutes, vagrants, mendi- Houses of ill fame and assignation.

cants, street beggars, drunken or disorderly persons; to prohibit, prevent and suppress mock auctions and every kind of fraudulent game, devise or practice, and punish all persons managing, using, practicing or attempting to manage, use or practice the same, and all persons aiding in the management, use or practice thereof.

Games.

Unsound meats.

39th. To prohibit, prevent and suppress the sale of every kind of unsound, nauseous and unwholesome meat, poultry, fish, vegetables or other articles of food and provisions, and impure or spurious wines and spirituous liquors, and to punish all persons, who shall knowingly sell the same, or offer to keep the same for sale.

Gaming.

40th. To prohibit, restrain and prevent persons from gaming for money with cards, dice, billiards, nine or ten pin alleys, tables, ball alleys, wheels of fortune, boxes, machines or other instruments or devices whatsoever, in any grocery, store, shop or any other place in said city; to punish the persons keeping the building, instruments or means for such gaming, and compel the destruction of the same.

Lotteries.

41st. To prohibit, prevent and suppress all lotteries for the drawing or disposing of money or any other property whatsoever, and to punish all persons maintaining, directing or managing the same, or aiding in the maintenance, direction or management thereof.

Intoxicating liquors.

42d. To prohibit and prevent persons from selling or giving away ardent spirits or other intoxicating liquors to any child, apprentice or servant without the consent of his or her parent, guardian, master or mistress; to license and regulate the selling or giving away of any ardent spirits or other intoxicating liquors by any shop-keeper, trader, grocer, inn, hotel or tavern keeper, keeper of any ordinary saloon, recess, victualling or other house, or by any other person, in case the selling or giving away of ardent spirits and other intoxicating liquors, and licensing the sale thereof, shall hereafter be authorized by the laws of the State.

43d. To license and regulate solicitors of passengers or for baggage for the benefit of any hotel, tavern, public house, boat or railroad, also draymen, carmen, truckmen, porters, runners, drivers of cabs, hackney coaches, omnibusses, carriages, sleighs, express vehicles and vehicles of every other description used and employed for hire, and to fix and regulate the amount and rates of their compensation. **To license Porters and Runners.**

44th. To license and regulate auctioneers, hawkers, peddlers and pawn-brokers, and regulate auctions, hawking, peddling and pawn-brokerage; to license and regulate the peddling and hawking of fruits, nuts, cakes, refreshments, jewelry, merchandise, goods and other property whatsoever, by hand, hand-cart, show-case, show-stand or otherwise in the public streets. **Auctioneers, Peddlers, &c.**

45th. To prohibit and prevent, or license and regulate the public exhibition by itinerant persons, or companies, of natural or artificial curiosities, caravans, circuses, menageries, theatrical representations, concerts, musical entertainments, exhibitions of common showmen, and shows of any kind. **Public Exhibitions.**

46th. To license, regulate and restrain the keepers of hotels, taverns and other public houses, grocers and keepers of ordinaries, saloons and victualling or other houses or places for furnishing meals, food or drink. **Hotels, &c,**

47th. To license and regulate butchers; to license and regulate or suppress hucksters, and to license and regulate the keepers of shops, stalls, booths or stands at markets or any other place in said city, for the sale of any kind of meat, fish, poultry, vegetables, food or provisions. **Butchers, Provision Dealers, &c.**

48th. To license and regulate keepers of billiard tables, pin alleys, nine or ten pin alleys, but not for the purpose of gaming. **Billiards and Pin Alleys.**

49th. To license and regulate public bath houses or bath rooms on land, and any public floating bath houses, bath rooms or vessels on the Detroit River. **Bath Houses.**

50th. To establish and regulate an efficient system of police for the good government of said city; to appoint, on the re- **Police.**

6

commendation of the Mayor or acting Mayor, policemen and watchmen, who shall possess and exercise the same powers, as conservators of the peace, which township Constables, under the general laws of this State, possess, and to prescribe and regulate their further powers and duties, and fix their compensation. Said policemen and watchmen may be removed at any time by the Common Council, on the recommendation of the Mayor or acting Mayor.

Removal of Policemen.

Weighers and Guagers.

51st. To appoint one or more inspectors, measurers, weighers and guagers of articles to be measured, inspected, weighed and guaged; to prescribe and regulate their powers and duties, fees and compensation.

Bread.

52d. To direct and regulate the weight and quality of bread, the size of the loaf, and the inspecting thereof.

Inspection of Wood, &c.

53d. To direct and regulate the inspecting and measuring of wood, lumber, shingles, timber, posts, stones, heading and all building materials; the inspecting, measuring and weighing of coke and all kinds of coal; the inspecting and weighing of hay; the inspecting of vegetables, fresh, dried, smoked, salted, pickled and other meat, or fish, poultry, butter, lard and other food or provisions to be sold at wholesale or retail; the inspecting and weighing of flour, meal, pork, beef and all other food or provisions, and salt, to be sold in half-barrels, barrels, casks, hogsheads, boxes or other packages; and the inspecting and guaging of oils, wines, whisky and other spirituous liquors, to be sold at wholesale or retail, or in kegs, half-barrels, barrels, casks, hogsheads or other vessels: *Provided*, that nothing herein contained shall be construed to authorize the inspecting, measuring, weighing or guaging of any article herein enumerated, which is to be shipped beyond the limits of this State, except at the request of the owner thereof or of the agent having charge of the same.

Proviso.

Weights and Measures.

54th. To regulate the weights and measures to be used in said city, and compel every merchant, retailer, trader and dealer in merchandise, groceries, provisions or property of any description which is sold by measure or weight, to use weights and measures to be sealed by the City Sealer, and to be subject to his inspection and alteration, so as to be made conformable to the standard of weights and measures established by the general laws of the State.

55th. To provide for the protection and care of paupers, and to prohibit and prevent all persons from bringing in vessels or in any other mode to said city, from any other port or place, any pauper or other person likely to become a charge upon said city, and to punish therefor. **Paupers.**

56th. To provide for the burial of strangers and poor deceased persons; to regulate the burial of the dead and the registration of births and deaths, and to order and compel the keeping and returning of bills of mortality by physicians, sextons and others. **Burial of Paupers, &c.** **Births, Deaths, &c.**

57th. To provide for taking a census of the inhabitants of said city, whenever the Common Council may see fit, and to direct and regulate the same; to provide for calling meetings of the inhabitants of said city by public notice thereof, fixing the time and place of meeting, and to regulate the ringing of bells. **Census.** **Public Meetings.**

58th. To erect and provide for the erection of a City Hall and all needful buildings and offices for the use of the corporation or of its officers, and to control and regulate the same. **Public Buildings.**

59th. To establish and organize and maintain an Alms-House Department, to purchase the necessary grounds, and erect and provide for erecting the necessary buildings therefor, either within or without the city limits. **Alms House Department.**

60th. To establish and build jails, work houses and houses of correction for the confinement of offenders; to erect and provide for erecting the necessary buildings therefor, and control and regulate the same; to appoint all necessary officers for taking charge of the same and of persons confined therein; to prescribe their powers and duties, and provide for their removal from office and the filling of vacancies, **Jails, Work Houses and Houses of Correction.**

Imprisonment. 61st. To imprison and confine in said jails, work houses and houses of correction, at hard labor or otherwise, all persons liable to be imprisoned or confined under this act or any ordinance of the Common Council, or lawfully committed thereto by any court or magistrate, as herein provided. Any court or magistrate in the City of Detroit or the County of Wayne may commit to any work house or house of correction of said city, instead of the jail of Wayne County, any person convicted of an offence against the general laws of the State, now or hereafter punishable by imprisonment in the jail of Wayne County. Any court of competent jurisdiction of the State of Michigan may, in its discretion, commit any male under sixteen or female under fourteen years of age to any work house or house of correction of said city, instead of the State prison, who shall be convicted of any crime now or hereafter punishable by imprisonment in the State prison, whenever in the opinion of the court the welfare of the public and of the convict will be promoted thereby. All expenses attending the confinement of any person sentenced to be committed to any work house or house of correction of said city for any offence against the general laws of the State, now or hereafter punishable by imprisonment in the State prison, shall be paid by the State Treasurer quarter-yearly, on the certificate of the City Controller that such expenses have been incurred. All expenses attending the confinement of any person sentenced to be committed to any work house or house of correction of said city for any offence against the general laws of the State, now or hereafter punishable by imprisonment in the State prison, shall be paid quarter-yearly by the Treasurer of the County in which the offender was tried and convicted, upon the certificate of the City Controller that such expenses have been incurred.

Speed of cars. 62d. To prescribe and regulate the speed of cars and engines on railroads within the limits of said city.

63d. To authorize the Mayor to grant issue and revoke licenses in all cases where licenses may be granted and issued under this act and the ordinances of the Common Council; to direct the manner of issuing and registering the same, and to prescribe the sum of money to be paid therefor into the treasury of the corporation. No license shall be granted for more than one year, and the person receiving the same shall, before the issuing thereof, execute a bond to the corporation in such sum as the Common Council may prescribe, with one or more sufficient sureties, conditioned for a faithful observance of the charter of the corporation and the ordinances of the Common Council, and otherwise conditioned as the Common Council may prescribe. The Mayor may inquire into the sufficiency of the sureties in such bond by an examination under oath as to their property and responsibility, which oath may be administered by him. The depositions of the surety shall be reduced to writing, be signed by him, certified by the Mayor, annexed to and filed with the bond to which it relates, in the office of the Clerk of the City. Licenses by Mayor.

64th. To assess, levy and collect taxes for the purposes of the corporation upon all property made taxable by law for State purposes, which taxes shall be liens upon the property taxed till paid; to make regulations for assessing, levying and collecting the same, and to sell the property taxed to pay the taxes thereon. Taxes.

65th. To appropriate money, provide for the payment of the debt and expenses of the said city, and make regulations concerning the same. Appropriation of money

66th. To punish all offenders for violations of or offences against this act or any ordinance of the Common Council enacted under this or any other act of the Legislature, by holding to bail for good behavior, by imposing fines, penalties, forfeitures and costs, and by imprisonment in the jail of Wayne County, any jail, work house, house of correction or alms house of said city, or by either, in the discretion of the court or magistrate before whom conviction may be had. If only a fine, penalty or forfeiture be imposed, together with the costs, the offender may be sentenced to be imprisoned Punishment of offenders.

until the payment thereof, for a term not exceeding six months. All punishments for offences against the ordinances of the Common Council shall be prescribed in the ordinance creating or specifying the offence to be punished; and no penalty or forfeiture shall exceed one thousand dollars, no fine shall exceed five hundred dollars, and no imprisonment shall exceed the period of two years.

Employment of prisoners. 67th. To employ all persons confined for the non-payment of any fine, penalty, forfeiture or costs, or for any offence under this act or any ordinance of the Common Council, in the jail of Wayne County or any jail, work house, house of correction or alms house of said city, at work and labor, either within or without the same, or upon the streets of said city, or any public work under the control of the Common Council; to allow any person thus confined for the non-payment of any fine, penalty, forfeiture or costs, to pay and discharge the same by such work and labor, and to fix the value and rates of such work and labor.

Printing. 68th. To provide for printing and publishing all matters required to be printed and published under this act or by order of the Common Council, in such manner as said Common Council may prescribe.

Public peace. 69th. To provide for maintaining the peace, order and good government of the City of Detroit.

Wards. 70th. The Common Council shall have power to subdivide the City of Detroit into wards.

Purchase real estate. 71st. The Common Council shall have power to purchase and sell real estate for the use of said corporation, for corporate purposes, and to execute mortgages on the same, for any balance which may remain unpaid on the purchase money paid for such real estate. They shall also have power to purchase and control land for cemetery purposes, either within or without the corporation limits of said city.

CHAPTER VI.

RECORDER'S COURT.

SECTION 1. There shall be a municipal court in and for the City of Detroit, to be called "The Recorder's Court," which shall be a court of record. Recorder's Court, Court of Record.

SEC. 2. The Recorder of said city shall be the Judge of said court, but in case of his absence from the city, inability to attend, or a vacancy in his office, one of the Judges of the Circuit Court, to be previously designated by the Recorder or the Common Council, shall be the Judge of said court, and, as such, have and exercise all the powers and duties of said Recorder until he shall resume his office, or such vacancy be filled. Recorder to be Judge, &c.

SEC. 3. There shall be a Clerk of said court, as before provided in this act, whose duty it shall be to keep a true record of the proceedings of said court in proper books to be provided therefor, and file and safely keep all books and papers belonging or pertaining to said court. He shall sign and seal all writs and process issuing from said court, and shall have power generally, to administer oaths and take affidavits. Clerk of Court, his duty and powers.

SEC. 4. The Sheriff of Wayne County and his deputies shall attend the sittings of said court, and it shall be their duty, and they shall have power to execute, under the direction of the Sheriff, all lawful precepts and commands of said court, and serve and execute all lawful writs and process issuing therefrom. Sheriff and deputy to attend Recorder's court.

SEC. 5. The said Recorder's Court shall have original and exclusive jurisdiction of all prosecutions and proceedings in behalf of the people of this State for crimes, misdemeanors and offences arising under the laws of this State and committed within the corporate limits of the City of Detroit, except in cases cognizable by the Police Court of the City of Detroit, or by the Justices of the Peace of the said city; and shall have power to issue all lawful writs and process, and to Jurisdiction of Recorder's court.

do all lawful acts which may be necessary and proper to carry into complete effect the powers and jurisdiction given by this act, and especially to issue all writs and process, and to do all acts which the Circuit Courts of this State, within their respective jurisdictions, may, in like cases, issue and do

Proviso.

by the laws of this State: *Provided*, That this section shall not be construed to prevent the grand jury for the County of Wayne from inquiring into and presenting indictments, as heretofore, for crimes and offences committed within the

2d Proviso.

limits of said city: *Provided, further*, That this act shall not in any way affect the jurisdiction of the Circuit Court for the County of Wayne over any case now pending in said court, nor the validity of any recognizance as heretofore made to said court.

Prosecutions, how commenced.

SEC. 6. Prosecutions in the Recorder's Court, for crimes, misdemeanors and offences arising under the laws of this State and within the jurisdiction of said court, may be either by information, complaint or indictment.

Form of information and compl'ts.

SEC. 7. Such informations and complaints shall be in the name of the People of the State of Michigan, shall be signed by the Prosecuting Attorney, shall be verified by the oath of the Prosecuting Attorney or of some complaining witness, and shall have thereon endorsed the names of the witnesses, as is required in cases of indictments, and shall have, in the statement of the offence or offences charged, the same preciseness and fullness in matters of substance, as is required in

Contents.

indictments in like cases in the courts of this State, and the same may be amended in like manner as is provided in

Joinder of offences.

cases of indictments. Different offences, or different degrees of the same offence, may be joined in one information or complaint, in all cases where the same might be joined by

Rights of defendants.

different courts in one indictment; and in all cases, a defendant or defendants shall have the same rights in all subsequent pleadings and proceedings as he or they would have, if prosecuted for the same offence by indictment.

SEC. 8. No information or complaint shall be filed against any person for either of the crimes of treason, murder, arson, rape or perjury, unless the same shall first be laid before the Judge of said court, and he shall thereon endorse a direction that the same shall be filed. Information or complai'ts in certain cases.

SEC. 9. When an offence consists of different degrees, the defendant or defendants may be found guilty of any degree of the offence inferior to the one charged in the information or complaint, or of any attempt to commit the same. Degrees of offences.

Sec. 10. All provisions of law relative to the joinder of persons or offences in one indictment, and relative to subsequent pleadings and proceedings in cases of indictment, in either the court of original or appellate jurisdiction, or in the execution of any sentence, shall be applicable, so far as may be, to prosecutions by information or complaint under this act, for offence against the laws of the State. General laws of State to apply.

SEC. 11. Said Recorder's Court shall have full jurisdiction and authority to control and enforce all recognizances lawfully taken by said court or by the Judge thereof, or by any other court, judge or magistrate, to compel any person or persons to appear before said Recorder's Court, and there to answer and do according to the terms thereof, and whenever default shall be made in any such recognizance, such default shall be duly entered of record in said Recorder's Court, and thereafter said court shall, upon motion of Prosecuting Attorney, summarily enter judgment against all the parties liable on said recognizance for the full amount thereof: *Provided, however*, That any person against whom such judgement may have been entered shall have the right to apply to the court within twenty days after the rendition of such judgment, for the vacation of the same for good cause shown thereon, and said court may thereupon, in its discretion, vacate such judgment on such terms as it may deem just. Execution shall be awarded and executed upon said judgment in like manner as is provided in personal actions. Jurisdiction of recognizance. Proviso.

Form of recognizance.

SEC. 12. All such recognizances as are mentioned in the preceding section may be in the usual form, or may contain a further clause, authorizing said Recorder's Court, upon default in said recognizances, summarily to enter judgment upon the same, against the several parties liable thereon, for the full amount of such recognizance.

Indictments presented to Circuit Court for Wayne to be certified to Recorder's Court.

SEC. 13. All indictments for offences committed within the limits of the City of Detroit, which may be found and presented to the Circuit Court for the County of Wayne, by the grand jury of said county, shall be forthwith certified and transmitted by the Clerk of said Circuit Court to said Recorder's Court, and thereupon said Recorder's Court shall have a full and complete jurisdiction of said indictments, as if the same had been originally presented to said Recorder's Court, and shall have full power to take all further proceedings thereon.

Pros. Attor'y for Wayne County to act for people in Recorder's Court.

SEC. 14. The Prosecuting Attorney for the County of Wayne shall appear and act for the people of the State of Michigan, in said Recorder's Court, in all cases arising under the laws of this State, and he shall render to said court, in writing and on oath, at the last term thereof in each year, an annual account of all moneys collected or received by him as the prosecuting officer of said court.

To render account.

Recorder's powers in case of habeas corpus.

SEC. 15. The Judge of said Recorder's Court shall possess the same power to grant writs of habeas corpus returnable before himself, and to adjudicate thereon, and do all acts in vacation touching any suit or proceeding in said court, as is now or may be possessed by the Circuit Courts of the State, in matters before said Circuit Courts.

Powers of Judge at Chambers.

SEC. 16. The Judge of the Recorder's Court shall have all such powers and authority at chambers touching any suit or proceeding in said Recorder's Court, as the Judges of the Circuit Courts now have or may have in like suits or proceedings before said Circuit Courts.

Rules of court, how made.

SEC. 17. The said Recorder's Court shall have power to make rules for regulating the practice and conducting the business thereof, and to alter, amend, or repeal the same, in its discretion.

SEC. 18. Said Recorder's Court shall devise its own seal, at the expense of said city, and a description thereof, attested by the Clerk of said court, shall be deposited in the office of the Controller. Seal.

SEC. 19. All writs and process issuing from said Recorder's Court, on complaints under the city ordinances, shall be directed to the Marshal or any Constable of said city, and may be served and executed by the officers to whom the same are directed, at any place within the limits of this State; and all writs and process for offences under the general laws of the State shall be directed to the Sheriff, shall run "in the name of the people of the State of Michigan," be sealed with the seal of the court, signed by the Clerk of said court, dated on the day on which the same may issue, and tested in the name of the Recorder of said city. Writs to whom directed and by whom and when served, form of, &c.

SEC. 20. All prosecutions for offences in said Recorder's Court, arising under this act or under any ordinance or regulation of the Common Council, shall be in the name of the people of the State of Michigan, and be commenced by filing with the Clerk of said court a complaint in writing in the form of an affidavit, duly sworn to before said Clerk and subscribed by the person making the complaint, and having endorsed thereon the proper jurat of said Clerk; and it shall be deemed sufficient to set forth in said complaint the offence complained of according to its substance. The trial shall be had and determined upon said complaint and upon pleadings which may be amended, in the same manner as indictments and pleadings under the general laws of the State. Prosecutions, how commenced. Trial.

SEC. 21. In case of a vacancy in the office of Attorney, his absence or inability to attend, said Recorder's Court may designate a suitable person to discharge the duties of said Attorney, until such vacancy be filled according to the provisions of this act, or he shall resume his office; and the person thus designated shall receive for his services a reason- Proceedings in case of vacancy in office of Attorney.

able compensation, to be paid by the County of Wayne, and fixed and determined by the Board of Auditors of said county.

Recorder's Court, terms of

SEC. 22. There shall be a term of said Recorder's Court once in each month, which shall commence on the first Monday thereof, and may be continued or adjourned from time to time, as long as said court may deem necessary for the transaction of its business; and if from any cause the Judge of said court shall be unable to hold the same on the first day of a term, the Clerk thereof shall have power to open said court, and adjourn it from day to day, until the Judge shall be able to attend, and in such case all prosecutions, proceedings and matters pending in said court, shall stand continued, until such Judge can hold said court.

Adjournm'nt of, &c.

Exclusive cognizance of

SEC. 23. Said Recorder's Court shall also have exclusive cognizance of all offences against any ordinances of the Common Council of the City of Detroit.

Writ of error to Supreme Court.

SEC. 24. All the proceedings of said Recorder's Court, at any time before or after final judgment or sentence, may be removed to the Supreme Court by writ of error or other process, in the same manner that like proceedings, may, by law, be removed to the Supreme Court from the Circuit Courts of the State, and the Supreme Court shall proceed to adjudicate thereon in the same manner as on proceedings removed from said Circuit Courts.

City Attorn'y to collect fines and penalties.

SEC. 25. It shall be the duty of the City Attorney to collect all fines and penalties imposed for offences under this act or any ordinance or regulation of the Common Council of said city, which shall be reported in writing by the Clerk of said court, at the close of each term thereof, to said Common Council, and immediately after their collection or receipt by the City Attorney, shall be paid by him to the Treasurer of said city.

Records open for inspection.

SEC. 26. The Common Council of said city and the Board of Auditors of Wayne County, or any committee thereof appointed for the purpose, may at all reasonable times inspect the records and papers of said Recorder's Court, and the Clerk thereof shall give them, when requested, any information within his power or knowledge concerning such records and papers, and concerning all fines and penalties imposed by said court.

SEC. 27. The City of Detroit shall be liable for all reasonable costs and expenses and board of prisoners incurred in prosecutions for offences and proceedings in said Recorder's Court, arising under this act, or any ordinance or regulation of the Common Council of said city; and the County of Wayne shall be liable for all reasonable costs and expenses and board of prisoners incurred in prosecutions for offences and proceedings in said court, arising under the general laws of the State; but if there be a conviction and sentence of confinement in any work house or house of correction of said city for any offence now or hereafter punishable by imprisonment in the State prison, the expenses attending the confinement of the prisoner after sentence shall be paid by the State Treasurer quarter-yearly, on the certificate of the City Controller that such expenses have been incurred.

City liable for expense of Board of prisoners in certain cases.

County liable for expenses in other cases

SEC. 28. The salary to be paid to the Recorder shall be the same as is allowed, or may be from time to time allowed, to the Circuit Judge of the State, and shall be paid by the State, in the same manner as the Circuit Judges are paid. The Clerk of the Recorder's Court shall be paid by the City of Detroit, such salary as the Common Council may prescribe.

Salary of Recorder—of Clerk.

SEC. 29. Any person liable to be imprisoned or confined under this act or any ordinance or regulation of the Common Council of said city, may be so imprisoned or confined in the jail of Wayne County, and it shall be the duty of the keeper of said jail to receive and safely keep therein all persons thus subject to imprisonment or confinement, until legally discharged therefrom.

Prisoners may be imprisoned in County jail.

SEC. 30. Any law of this State for the safe keeping of prisoners in a county jail, or for preventing or punishing their escape or the aiding of them to escape, or any other act detrimental to their safe keeping in a county jail, shall

General laws to apply.

apply to any jail, work house or house of correction, established and provided under this act by the City of Detroit for the imprisonment or confinement of offenders, in the same manner and to the same effect as to the county jail.

Certain punishments to be prescr bed by Common Council.

SEC. 31. Punishments not herein prescribed for offences against this act, and for offences against the ordinances and regulations of the Common Council, shall be prescribed by said Common Council.

Challenges of Jurors.

SEC. 32. In all jury trials in said Recorder's Court, the person or persons on trial shall have the same right of challenge and other rights and benefits extended by law to persons on trial by a jury in criminal cases before the Circuit Courts of the State, subject to the provisions of this act.

Trial by jury.

SEC. 33. In all trials upon indictments, the person or persons on trial shall be tried by a jury, unless the right to a jury trial be, with consent of the court, waived. In all trials for offences against this act or any ordinance or regulation of the Common Council of said city, the person or persons on trial shall be tried by the court, unless he or they shall request to be tried by a jury. Juries shall be obtained, summoned, drawn and sworn as hereinafter provided.

Selection of persons to serve as jurors.

SEC. 34. The Assessor of said city, at the time herein appointed to review the assessment rolls in each year, shall select from them, when completed, a list of three hundred persons to serve as jurors in all cases where juries may be required under this act or any ordinance or regulation of the Common Council; and the persons thus selected shall be qualified electors of the City of Detroit, shall be of fair character and sound judgment and understanding, and, so far as practicable, such as were not actually drawn, or did not serve as jurors during the preceding year. If said Assessor shall refuse or neglect to return the list of jurors, as above provided, the Judge of the Recorder's Court shall have power to compel him to make such return. For every day that said Assessor shall neglect or refuse to make such returns, after the time prescribed in this section, he shall forfeit the

Penalty on Assessor for neglect to return a list of jurors.

sum of one hundred dollars. Said list shall be signed by said Assessor, returned to the Clerk of said Recorder's Court and filed in his office.

SEC. 35. The Clerk of said court, on receiving said list, shall file it in his office, shall write the names of the persons thus selected on separate strips of paper of the same size and appearance as nearly as may be, shall fold up each of said strips of paper in the same manner, so as to conceal the name thereon, and deposit and preserve the same in a box to be called and labelled "jury box," and the persons whose names are thus returned and deposited in said jury box, shall be liable to serve as jurors for one year, and until another list shall be selected, returned and filed with said Clerk, and the names thereon deposited in said jury box in the manner aforesaid. Clerk's duties on receiving list.

SEC. 36. Before depositing in said jury box the names contained in any new list, the ballots deposited therein for the preceding year shall be taken out and destroyed, and it shall be the duty of the Judge of said court to attend and be present with the Clerk, when the ballots, containing the names of persons to serve as jurors, are deposited in said jury box or taken out to be destroyed. Old ballots to be destroyed. New ballots to be put in jury box.

SEC. 37. At least ten days before any term of said Recorder's Court, at which jury trials may be had as above provided, the Clerk of said court shall draw from the jury box the names of as many persons as the Judge of said court may deem necessary, not less than fourteen, nor more than twenty-four, to serve as petit jurors in said court; and at least two days before such drawing, the said Clerk shall give notice to the Judge of said court and to the Sheriff of the day and hour when such drawing shall take place. Drawing Petit Jurors.

SEC. 38. At the time so appointed, it shall be the duty of said Judge and of the Sheriff of Wayne County or some Deputy Sheriff to attend at the Clerk's office and witness said drawing of jurors, and if neither said Judge, Sheriff or Deputy Sheriff be present at the appointed time, the Clerk Judges and Sheriff of Wayne County to attend drawing.

may adjourn such drawing to some certain hour on the next day, of which adjournment he shall forthwith give notice to said Judge and Sheriff.

Proceedings on drawing jurors.

SEC. 39. If at the time first appointed for such drawing, or at the adjourned time therefor, either said Judge, Sheriff or Deputy Sheriff shall be present, the Clerk shall proceed in such drawing as follows: he shall shake the jury box, so as fairly to mix the slips of paper deposited therein; shall then draw from said box publicly and in the presence of the officer or officers attending, as many strips of paper containing the names of jurors written thereon, as may have been ordered by said Judge, and one of the attending officers shall keep a minute of such drawing, in which he shall enter the name of every strip of paper drawn, before any other such strip be drawn. If, after drawing the whole number required, the name of any person shall appear to have been drawn who is insane or dead, or has removed from the City of Detroit, to the knowledge of said Clerk or any attending officer, and entry of such fact shall be made on the minute of the drawing, the strip of paper containing his name shall be destroyed, and another name shall then be drawn in the place of that destroyed, and entered on the minute of the drawing, and like proceedings shall be had as often as necessary, until the whole number of jurors required shall be drawn.

Minute of drawing jurors to be filed.

SEC. 40. The said minute of the drawing shall then be signed by the Clerk of said court and the attending officers, and filed by the Clerk in his office, and he shall immediately make out a *venire facias* and deliver the same to the Sheriff of Wayne County, which shall command him or any of his deputies to summon the persons therein named to be and appear in said court, at the terms thereof for which they were drawn, to serve as petit jurors, and not depart the same until discharged, under such penalty as the court may impose.

Venire facias. Who to serve.

Venire facias how served and returned.

SEC. 41. Said *venire facias* shall be served at least three days before the term of the court therein specified, by giving personal notice to each person therein named or by leaving a written notice at his place of residence, with some person of proper age, and return thereof shall be made to said court at its opening, specifying those who were summoned, and the manner in which each person was notified.

SEC. 42. Said court shall impose a fine on each person duly summoned to attend as a juror, who shall, without reasonable cause, neglect to attend, not exceeding five dollars for each day's non-attendance and neglect; but all persons who, under the general laws of the State, are exempted or may be excused from serving as jurors in the Circuit Courts, shall be exempted and may be excused from serving as jurors in said Recorder's Court.

Fines for neglect of jurors to attend.

Exemption.

SEC. 43. The Clerk of said court shall destroy the ballots of all persons excused from serving as jurors, on the ground of being exempted by law from such service; and the ballots of persons who did not appear and serve, which shall not have been destroyed, shall be returned to the jury box.

Proceedings when jurors excused.

SEC. 44. The ballots of persons who shall attend and serve as jurors, shall be enclosed by the Clerk in an envelope under seal, or deposited by him in a separate box and preserved; and if, at any subsequent drawing of a jury, a sufficient number of ballots shall not remain in the jury box to furnish the number of jurors required, after having drawn all the ballots therein, the ballots preserved by the Clerk as aforesaid shall be returned by him to the jury box and drawn in like manner as required above, until the required number of jurors is obtained.

Ballots of persons attending as jurors to be deposited in box.

SEC. 45. Whenever, for any cause, petit jurors shall not have been drawn or summoned to attend any term of said Recorder's Court, or a sufficient number of qualified jurors shall fail to appear, such court may, in its discretion, order a sufficient number of petit jurors to be forthwith drawn and summoned to attend such court; or said court may, by an order to be entered in its minutes, direct the Sheriff forthwith

Drawing jurors forthwith in certain cases.

to summon so many good and qualified men of said city to serve as such jurors, as the case may require.

Duties of Sheriff in summoning jurors and making return.

SEC. 46. The Sheriff, on receiving a list of jurors drawn pursuant to the preceding section, or a copy of the order therein mentioned, shall proceed, as soon as possible, to summon such jurors forthwith to attend such court, and make return to said court of his doings, in the same manner as in the case of a *venire facias*.

Talesmen.

SEC. 47. When there shall not be jurors enough present to form a panel in any case, said court may direct the Sheriff to summon a sufficient number of persons having the qualifications of jurors, to complete the panel, from among the by-standers or the neighboring citizens; and the Sheriff shall immediately summon the number so ordered and return their names to said court.

General laws applicable to further proceedings.

SEC. 48. In all further proceedings touching jury trials, their incidents and all matters connected therewith, said Recorder's Court shall be governed, in the same manner as the Circuit Courts of the State, by the general laws thereof, which, so far as the same may apply, are hereby made applicable to said Recorder's Court, its officers and all proceedings therein, subject to the provisions of this act.

Clerk to report to Common Council.

Report what to contain.

SEC. 49. The Clerk of said court, on the first day of January in each year, or as soon thereafter as practicable, shall make to the Common Council a report in writing, duly certified by him, showing the whole number of prosecutions by indictment, which number shall be also classified by the name or description of the offence; the whole number of prosecutions for offences against this act or the ordinances and regulations of the Common Council, which shall be also classified in like manner, so far as practicable; the whole number of prosecutions, convictions, acquittals, cases dismissed and discontinued, and cases pending; the whole number of sentences passed; the whole number punished by fines and penalties; the whole number punished by imprisonment and confinement, which shall be also classified according to the prison, jail or other place of imprisonment or confinement; and the whole number held to bail for good behavior and to keep the peace; and said report shall be published in the daily newspaper published by the printer for the city.

SEC. 50. The provisions of this chapter shall not go into effect until the second Tuesday in January, 1858; and the provisions of the present Charter of said city, relative to the Mayor's Court, shall continue in full force and effect until the Recorder's Court is organized, under this act.

Provisions of this Chap. to go into effect on 2d Tuesday in Janu'ry, 1858.

CHAPTER VII.

OPENING, ALTERING AND CLOSING STREETS.

SECTION 1. The Common Council of the City of Detroit shall have full power to lay out, establish, open, extend, widen, straighten, alter, close, vacate or abolish any highways, streets, avenues, lanes, alleys, public grounds or spaces in said city, whenever they shall deem it a necessary public improvement, and private property may be taken therefor; but the necessity for using such property, the just compensation to be made for the same, and the damages arising to any person from the making of said improvement shall be ascertained by a jury of twelve freeholders residing in said city.

Powers of Common Council as to streets.

SEC. 2. Whenever the Common Council shall deem any such improvement necessary, they shall so declare by resolution, which shall be drawn by the City Attorney, and in said resolution shall describe the contemplated improvement; and if they intend to take private property therefor, they shall declare such intention and describe such property in said resolution, with particularity sufficient for an ordinary conveyance thereof; and further declare that they will, on some day to be named in said resolution, apply to the Recorder's Court of said city for the drawing of a jury to ascertain the necessity for using the property intended to be taken, if it be in-

Resolution declaring improvement necessary—what to contain.

tended to take any for such improvement, to ascertain the just damages and compensation which any person may be entitled to, if such intended improvement be made, and to apportion and assess such damages and compensation to and upon all lots, premises and subdivisions thereof which will be benefitted by such improvement; and the time to be named for applying to said court, shall be on a day subsequent to the required publication of said resolution.

Notice of intended improvement—how given.

SEC. 3. The Common Council shall give notice of the intended improvement and of their intended application to said court, by causing a copy of said resolution, certified by the Clerk of the City, to be published for four successive weeks in the official daily newspaper of the city and one other daily newspaper published in said city, and the Marshal shall also give notice of said resolution by delivering a notice thereof, with a copy of the same annexed, to the owner or owners or agent of any private property intended to be taken, if they can be found in said city, which notice shall be directed to them, or, if they cannot be found, by leaving the same at their place of residence in said city with some person of proper age. If they or their place of residence cannot be found and such property be occupied, said notice and copy of said resolution shall be served by delivering the same to the occupant or occupants, or by leaving the same at their place of residence within said city with some person of proper age; but if the owner or owners or agent of such property or their place of residence cannot be found and it be not occupied, or, if it be occupied, but they, their place of residence and that of the occupant or occupants cannot be found, or, if the owner or owners, occupant or occupants be unknown or non-residents of said city, then, in either of such cases, notice of said resolution may be given by posting the same with the copy of said resolution in some conspicuous place upon the property intended to be taken. The Marshal shall give notice of said resolution as above directed, and make return of his doings and of the manner of giving said

Upon whom served.

Return of services.

notice as soon as practicable after the passage thereof, which return shall be made to said Recorder's Court, at least six days before the day appointed in said resolution for the hearing of said application, and all persons interested therein, after notice given in the manner aforesaid, shall take notice of and be bound by all subsequent proceedings, without any further notices, except as herein otherwise provided. When and where made.

SEC. 4. The Clerk of the City shall deliver to the City Attorney a certified copy of said resolution of the Common Council, whose duty it shall be to appear in said court and make the application therein referred to, and conduct all further proceedings thereon in behalf of the Common Council. Certifi'd copy of resolution to be served on City Attorney.

SEC. 5. Upon the day designated in said resolution, or some other day to be appointed by the court, and on filing a copy of said resolution and an affidavit showing the required publication thereof, the Marshal shall attend said court and write down the names of twenty-four disinterested freeholders residing in said city, and who shall be approved by the court as such disinterested freeholders and residents, and as qualified to serve. Jurors.

SEC. 6. Said court shall then issue a writ of summons, commanding the Marshal to summon said twenty-four persons to be and appear in said court to serve as jurors, on some day to be named therein, which shall not be less than seven days after the issuing thereof. The Marshal shall serve such summons at least three days before the return day thereof, and make return in the same manner as in the case of a summons for petit jurors of said court; and the persons thus summoned shall be bound to attend said court and serve until discharged, and said court shall impose upon them a fine not exceeding five dollars for each day's non-attendance in court or neglect to serve; but they may be exempted and excused by the court from serving for the same reasons for which petit jurors may be exempted or excused. Summoning jurors.

SEC. 7. The names of the jurors in attendance and who do not claim to be exempted or are not excused from serving,

Drawing jury.

shall then be written by the Clerk of the court on separate slips of paper, of equal size and appearance, as near as practicable, and be deposited by him in a box having a lid or cover. He shall then shake said box, so as thoroughly to mix said slips of paper, and shall then draw impartially, openly and in the presence of the court, so many of the slips of paper or ballots containing names written theron, one after another, as shall be sufficient to form a jury. The right of challenge shall be allowed as in civil cases under the laws of the State.

In case of insufficiency of ballots other persons to be summoned.

SEC. 8. If, in consequence of jurors being exempted, excused or set aside, there shall not be in the box any ballots or a sufficient number of ballots from which to draw the jury, the Marshal shall forthwith, under the order of the court, summon such number of persons as the court shall deem necessary, and may order to be and appear in said court to serve as jurors, and the persons thus summoned shall be returned, be bound to attend said court and serve, and be competent to form the jury, in the same manner and to the same effect as those first summoned.

First 12 appearing and approved to be jury and be sworn.

SEC. 9. The first twelve persons who shall appear as their names are drawn and called by the Clerk, or who are called by him when all the ballots have been drawn from the box, and shall be approved by the court as qualified, shall be the jury, and be sworn to discharge their duties faithfully and according to the best of their abilities. Said court shall then instruct said jury as to their duties and the law applicable to the case, and deliver to them a copy of the resolution of the Common Council, as filed in said court, certified by the Clerk of said court; and the City Attorney shall give said jury legal advice and counsel concerning their duties whenever requested.

Instructions to jury by Court and Attorney.

Jury to view.

SEC. 10. The jury shall go to the place of the intended improvement and upon or as near as practicable to any property intended to be taken and described in said resolution, or as the case may be, which will be damaged or benefitted, if the intended improvement be made.

SEC. 11. Said jury shall then ascertain the necessity for using the property intended to be taken, if it be intended to take any for such improvement, and if they shall find in the affirmative, they shall next determine the just damages and compensation to be paid to the owner or owners of any property intended to be taken for, or that may be damaged by, the intended improvement, and award to the owner or owners thereof such damages and compensation as they shall deem just. If such property shall be subject to a valid mortgage, lease and agreement, or to either, and such facts shall be made to appear to the jury, then said jury shall apportion and award to the owners of such property, the parties in interest to such mortgage, lease and agreement, or to either of them, such portions of the damages and compensation as they shall deem just. And in all cases where any such damage shall be awarded, except for the laying out, establishing, opening, widening, altering or vacating an alley or alleys, such damage shall be payable out of the city treasury, and the means therefor shall be raised from time to time, as may be necessary, with the general city taxes.

Duties of jury.

Certain damages payable out of City Treasury.

SEC. 12. In cases of the laying out, establishing, opening, widening, altering or vacating an alley or alleys, said jury shall further proceed to apportion the total damages and compensation to be paid for the proposed improvement among the lots of land, premises or subdivisions thereof, within the block in which the alley in question is situated, and which will be benefitted by the proposed improvement, apportioning and assessing the same upon the said lots, premises or subdivisions thereof, as near as may be, in proportion as the same will be benefitted by said improvement. The word "alley," as used in this chapter, shall be construed to mean only those ways or passages which bisect or divide the interior of a block. No alleys shall be opened, except upon a petition of the owners of a majority of the lots on the block or blocks to be intersected thereby, and upon security being given to indemnify the city against the expenses of opening said alleys.

Apportionment of damages among lots to be benefitted.

Definition of word "alley," of opening alley.

Report of jury.

SEC. 13. Said jury, after completing the aforesaid duties, shall then make in writing and each shall sign the report to said court of their doings, enclose the same in a sealed envelope and file it in the office of the Clerk of said court, within thirty days after they were sworn.

Report what to contain.

SEC. 14. In all cases where said jury shall find such improvement to be necessary, they shall state in their report the just damages and compensation ascertained and awarded by them to the owner of any private property or to any person claiming an interest therein by virtue of any valid mortgage, lease or agreement to which such property may be subject, together with the names of such owner or claimant, if known, and a description of the property intended to be taken. In case any damages and compensation be awarded to any person claiming an interest in such property, by virtue of a valid mortgage, lease or agreement to which such property may be subject, it shall be sufficient to state further in such case the name of such claimant, the date of such mortgage, lease or agreement, or assignment thereof, if there be any, by virtue of which such claimant has an interest in the property intended to be taken.

What further to contain.

SEC. 15. Said jury shall also, in the case provided for by section 12, state in their report what portions in amount of the total ascertained damages and compensation they have apportioned to and assessed upon any lot, premises or subdivision thereof, which will be benefitted by the intended improvement, together with the names of the owners thereof, if known, and a description of the same, and also what portion, if any, of the ascertained damages and compensation they have apportioned and assessed to the City of Detroit in the case above provided for.

Confirmation of report.

SEC. 16. Said report may be confirmed by said court at any term thereof, and the court shall appoint some day when it will consider said report and objections against the confirmation thereof on the part of all persons interested therein, whereof the City Attorney shall give notice by publishing the same in the official daily newspaper of said city and in one other daily newspaper published in said city, for six successive days, and he shall file in said court an affidavit of such publication before the time appointed for considering said report. Said objections shall be filed with the Clerk in writing, but may be argued, and the consideration of said report and objections may be adjourned from time to time, until said report be confirmed or otherwise disposed of as herein provided. Objection.

Report not to be annulled for matters of form.

SEC. 17. Said report shall not be annulled for objections as to matters of form; all objections shall be objections of law and to matters of substance, but the damages and compensation to be paid to any person, or the portions thereof apportioned to and assessed upon any lot of land, premises or subdivision thereof, may be inquired into, if objected to as being excessively large or small.

If no objections filed, report to be confirmed.

Proceedings if objections are filed.

SEC. 18. If no objections be filed, said report shall be confirmed; but if objections be filed, said court, after considering the same, shall in its discretion confirm or annul said report, or may refer it back to the same jury for the purpose of reviewing all matters and correcting all errors therein contained, and making any alteration thereof which said court may direct, or said jury may deem just or necessary, and thereon said jury shall review, correct or alter said report in manner aforesaid, and shall return and file the same with the Clerk of said court, within five days after said report was referred back to them as aforesaid, and thereupon said court shall confirm or annul said report.

New Jury to be summoned in certain cases.

SEC. 19. If said report be annulled, or the jury cannot agree, or from death, sickness or any other cause shall fail to make a report within the thirty days required above, the court may, on the application of the City Attorney, designate some day in term when another jury may be had, and such jury shall be obtained, drawn, summoned, returned, bound to attend and serve, have the same qualifications, be sworn, and, when sworn, have the same powers and duties as the first jury. The same proceedings, after they are sworn, shall be had by them and by and in said court, as provided for above, after the first jury is sworn.

Vacancy in jury, how supplied. SEC. 20. If any juror, after being sworn, shall die or from sickness be unable to discharge his duties, the court may appoint another person to serve in his place, who shall be sworn and shall have the like qualifications, powers and duties as those already sworn.

Appeal. SEC. 21. Any person to whom damages and compensation may be awarded for any of his property intended to be taken, or on account of the intended improvement, or to and upon whose property any portion of such damages and compensation may be apportioned and assessed, considering himself aggrieved, may appeal from the judgment of the Recorder's Court, confirming the report of the jury, to the Supreme Court by filing in writing with the Clerk of said Recorder's Court a notice of such appeal and specification of the errors complained of, within five days after the confirmation, and serving within the same time a copy of said notice and specification of errors on the City Attorney, and filing a bond in said Recorder's Court, to be approved by the Recorder, condition for the prosecution of said appeal and the payment of all costs that may be awarded against the appellant, in case the judgment of confirmation of the Recorder's Court be affirmed.

Notice of specification of errors.

Bond on appeal.

Condition.

Return to appeal. SEC. 22. In case of appeal as above, it shall be the duty of the Clerk of said Recorder's Court forthwith, or as soon as practicable, to transmit to the Supreme Court a certified copy of all the proceedings in the case, which may be filed in the office of any clerk of said court.

Duties of Supreme Court on appeal. SEC. 23. The Supreme Court, at any term thereof, shall, with the least practicable delay, hear and try the matter of said appeal, and may affirm or reverse the judgment of the Recorder's Court, confirming the report of the jury; but the same shall not be reversed for matter of form, nor for any errors, except errors of law, and only in regard to the appellant or appellants. The court shall give judgment for reasonable costs and expenses in the matter of said appeal and proceedings thereon to be taxed, and all costs and expenses awarded to the City of Detroit, in case of affirmation, shall be applied on and deducted from the damages and compensation, if any, to be paid to the appellant or appellants.

SEC. 24. If there be a reversal for any errors, which it is practicable for the Recorder's Court or said jury to correct with due regard to the public interest and rights of individuals, the proceedings shall be remanded to said Recorder's Court, with direction that such error be corrected. Said Recorder's Court, at any term thereof, or (as the case may be) said jury, under the direction of said court, shall correct such error, and thereupon the report of the jury shall be confirmed by said Recorder's Court, without any further right of appeal.

Remanding proceedings in certain cases.

SEC. 25. In every case of annullment of the report of the jury by the Recorder's Court, or reversal by the Supreme Court, the Common Council, in behalf of said city, may by resolution elect to pay the damages and compensation claimed by, or the assessment made upon the property of the objector, appellant or appellants. On filing a certified copy of said resolution in the Recorder's Court, within twenty days after the annullment or reversal, the report of said jury shall be reviewed and confirmed by said Recorder's Court as to all persons interested therein, except the objector, appellant or appellants, and without further right of appeal. If the Common Council do not elect, as above provided, all the proceedings shall be null and void, and no further proceedings shall be had, except in a case of reversal, when the proceedings may have been remanded to the Recorder's Court for the correction of certain errors, in which case such errors shall be corrected and the report of the jury confirmed, as above provided.

Common Council may elect in certain cases to pay damages.

SEC. 26. If the report of the jury be confirmed by the Recorder's Court in any case above provided for, or if the judgment of confirmation be affirmed on appeal to the

Confirmation of report to be final.

Supreme Court, such confirmation shall be final and conclusive as to all persons interested therein; and the damages and compensation apportionod to and assessed upon any lot of land, premises or subdivision thereof, according to said report as confirmed, shall be a lien thereon, from the time of the aforesaid confirmation until they are paid and satisfied.

Certified copy of proceedings to be filed and recorded.

Sec. 27. When the report of the jury shall have been thus finally confirmed, or the judgment of confirmation affirmed by the Supreme Court, the Clerk of the Recorder's Court shall prepare a certified copy, under the seal of the court, of the report of the jury as confirmed by the Recorder's Court and of the order of the court confirming the same, and the Clerk shall file said certified copy in the office of the Clerk of the City, who shall record the same at length in a book to be provided, used and known as a book of street records. Such certificd copy, such record, or a like copy made and certified by the Clerk of the Recorder's Court, shall in all courts and places be presumptive evidence of the matters therein contained and of the regularity of all proceedings from the commencement thereof, to the order of the court confirming the report of the jury.

Amounts to be paid to City Treas'er.

Sec. 28. The amounts apportioned to and assessed upon all lots of land, premises or subdivisions thereof for the benefits they will receive, shall be paid to the Treasurer of said city, in case of confirmation of the report of the jury as above provided, or in case the judgment of confirmation be affirmed by the Supreme Court, and may be collected, and said lots, premises or subdivisions thereof may be sold therefor in the same manner as in the case of collection or sale for assessments to pay the cost and expenses of paving streets.

Damages to be paid or tendered in sixty days.

Sec 29. Within sixty days after the confirmation of the report of the jury, or after the judgment of confirmation shall on appeal be affirmed, the Common Council shall pay or tender to the respective persons the several amounts of damages and compensation awarded to them, according to the report of the jury as confirmed, or elected as above provided for, to be paid by the Common Council; and in case any such person shall refuse the same, be unknown, or a non-resident of said city, or for any reason incapacitated from receiving his or her amount, or the right thereto be disputed or doubtful, the Common Council may deposit the amount awarded in such case, or elected to be paid by the Common Council, in the treasury of the city, to the credit of any person entitled thereto, and shall on demand pay the same over to any person competent and entitled to receive it.

Damages to be deposited in certain cases with Treasurer.

SEC. 30. Upon such payment, tender or deposit in the city treasury, the same shall become a public highway, and the Common Council may enter upon, take possession of and convert the same to the uses and purposes for which it has been taken. A certificate of the City Treasurer of such tender, payment or deposit, or record thereof in the book of street records, or certified copy of such record, shall in all courts and places be presumptive evidence of the facts therein stated, of the vesting of the fee of the property taken in the City of Detroit, and of the right of the Common Council to take possession of and convert the same to the uses for which it has been taken.

Upon payment, tender or deposit to become public highway.

SEC. 31. In all cases where any real estate, subject to any lease or agreement, shall be taken as aforesaid, all the covenants and stipulations contained therein shall cease, determine and be discharged, upon the final confirmation of the report of the jury, or upon the affirmation by the Supreme Court of the judgment of confirmation. If a part only of such real estate be taken, said covenants and stipulations shall cease, determine and be discharged only as to such part; and the Recorder's Court, on application of any party in interest to such lease or agreement, and after a notice thereof of eight days, in writing, to the other parties in interest, may appoint three disinterested residents and freeholders of said city, Commissioners to determine the rents and payments to be thereafter paid, and the covenants, stipulations or conditions thereafter to be performed under such lease or

Upon confirmation of report, stipulations in lease or agreements to cease.

Commiss'ers to apportion rents in certain cases.

agreement, in respect to the residue or part of such real estate not taken. Said Commissioners shall, before entering on their duties, take and subscribe an oath, to be administered by the court, faithfully to discharge their duties, which oath shall be filed in said court. Said three Commissioners shall make and sign a report in writing of their doings to said court, which shall be filed therein within thirty days after their appointment, and said report, on being confirmed by the court, shall be binding and conclusive on the parties in interest to such lease or agreement.

Duties of Commiss'ers.

Compensat'n of Jury.

SEC. 32. The Common Conncil shall pay said jury such compensation for their services, as they may deem just, and they shall have power to abandon or discontinue proceedings under this chapter in said Recorder's Court, at any time before the final confirmation of the report of the jury.

Common Council may abandon proceedings.

Commission on plan of city.

SEC. 33. For the purpose of introducing a greater uniformity in the laying out the land in said city into public streets and blocks, and to restrain persons from laying out such streets and blocks in a manner prejudicial to the interest of the city, there shall be constituted a Board of Commissioners, upon the plan of the city, consisting of three persons, to be appointed by the Common Council, on the nomination of the Mayor, and no land within the limits of said city shall be laid out into blocks and public streets, without the consent and approval of a majority of said Commissioners, in writing, entered upon a plan of said land so laid out, which plan, duly acknowledged, and with said approval in writing thereon endorsed, shall be recorded in the Register's Office for the County of Wayne: *Provided, however*, In cases where a parcel of land lies between parcels of land duly laid out by plats, now on record, where streets do not correspond in direction or size, the power of control shall not be so exercised over the platting of such intermediate parcel in order to produce such correspondence, as to essentially diminish their value.

Land not to be laid out into blocks and streets without consent of Commissioners.

Proviso.

SEC. 34. The City Clerk shall act as the Clerk of said Board, and plans for the approval of said Commissioners may be deposited with said Clerk for their action thereon, and if approved, a copy thereof shall be filed with said Clerk by the person making or laying out the same. Clerk of Board—plans to be deposited with Clerk

SEC. 35. Any plans for laying out into public streets and blocks, now existing in said city, and not acknowledged and recorded according to law, shall be of no validity until they receive the approval of said Commissioners, as herein before provided. Plans not acknowledged and recorded to be of no validity without approval of Comm'rs.

SEC. 36. If a vacancy occurrs in the office of said Commissioners, or either of them, it may be filled by the Common Council on the nomination of the Mayor. Vacancies, how filled.

SEC. 37. Said Commissioners shall receive no compensation for their services. No compensation.

CHAPTER VIII.

TAXATION AND FINANCE.

SEC. 1. The revenues and moneys of the corporation shall be divided in the following funds, viz: Funds.

1st. General Fund, which shall be appropriated to defray the expenses of the City of Detroit, for the payment of which out of some other fund, no provision is herein made. General Fund

2d. Contingent Fund, to defray the contingent expenses of said city. Contingent.

3d. Interest Fund, to pay the interest on the funded debt of said city. Interest.

4th. Sinking Fund, to pay the funded debt of said city. Sinking Fund

5th. Fire Department Fund, to defray the expenses of purchasing lots, erecting engine houses thereon, purchasing engines and other fire apparatus, and all other expenses necessary to maintain the Fire Department of said city. Fire Department Fund.

6th. Poor Fund, to defray the expenses of providing for and taking care of the poor of said city. Poor Fund.

General Road Fund. 7th. General Road Fund, to defray the expenses of repairing paved streets and alleys, and of grading, paving and improving the highways, streets and alleys of said city, in front of or adjacent to the property of the corporation.

District Road Fund. 8th. District Road Fund for each ward of said city, to defray the expenses of working, repairing, cleaning and improving the highways, streets and alleys in the ward for which such District Road Fund is constituted and raised.

Sewer Fund. 9th. Sewer Fund, to defray the expenses of constructing sewers and drains in said city.

Street Opening Fund. 10th. Street Opening Fund, to defray the expenses of opening, widening, vacating, altering, straightening, extending or abolishing any highways, streets or avenues in said city, under the provisions of chapter 7 of this act.

Street Paving Fund. 11th. Street Paving Fund, to defray the expenses of grading and paving, graveling, macadamising or planking highways, streets, alleys, side-walks and cross-walks in front of or adjacent to private property, and of putting curb-stones and culverts therein.

Public Building Fund. 12th. Public Building Fund, for purchasing real estate for the erection thereon of any public buildings, and to defray the expenses of erecting, repairing and preserving such public buildings as the Common Council is authorized to erect and maintain, and are not herein otherwise provided for, which fund shall from time to time, be divided into Special Building Funds, to defray the expenses of erecting, repairing and preserving the particular building or buildings for which such Special Building Fund may be constituted or raised.

Recorder's Court Fund. 13th. Recorder's Court Fund, to maintain the Recorder's Court.

Other Funds. 14th. Such other funds as the Common Council may constitute for special purposes, not inconsistent with, nor to be taken from any of the funds above constituted or raised.

Powers of Council to collect. SEC. 2. The Common Council shall have power annually, to levy, assess and collect taxes, not exceeding one per cent. on the assessed value of all real and personal estate in said city, made taxable by the laws of this State, in order to defray the expenses, and for the purposes for which the General Fund, Contingent Fund, Fire Department Fund, Poor Fund, General Road Fund and Recorder's Court Fund are constituted as above. Taxes for certain funds.

SEC. 3. The Common Council shall also have power annually to levy, assess and collect taxes on the assessed value of all real and personal estate in each ward of said city, made taxable by the laws of this State, in order to defray the expenses, and for the purposes for which the District Road Fund is constituted as above: *Provided*, That such taxes shall not exceed, in amount, the rates of township road or highway taxes as now or hereafter established by the laws of this State. For District Road Fund.

SEC. 4. The Common Council shall also have power annually to levy, assess and collect taxes, not exceeding thirty thousand dollars, on the assessed value of all real and personal estate in said city, made taxable by the laws of this State, in order to defray the expenses of constructing sewers, and for the purposes for which the Sewer Fund is constituted as above. For Sewer Fund.

SEC. 5. Before any taxes shall be levied, as aforesaid, for the purposes of the General Fund, Contingent Fund, General Road Fund, Street Opening Fund, District Road Fund, Fire Department Fund, Poor Fund, Sewer Fund, and Recorder's Court Fund, the Controller shall present to the Common Council in writing, his estimate of the amount of taxes, which, in his opinion, it may be necessary to raise for the ensuing year, for the purposes of said funds: shall state therein the amount estimated for the purposes of each of said funds, and also an estimate of the entire proposed expenditures for said year, whether the same are to be raised by tax, by loan, or by special assessment, and said estimate shall be published in the official paper of the city, and shall, at the same time, give to the Common Council any information in his power, and which they may request, concerning the finances Controller to present estimate.

of said city. The Common Council, after revising or altering said estimate, but not so as to exceed the aggregate taxes hereby authorized to be levied, shall direct the Mayor or acting Mayor to call a public meeting of the citizens of said city, to take into consideration the taxes proposed to be raised and specified in said estimate, by publishing notice thereof in one or more daily newspapers published in said city, for not less than three successive days, and posting the same in conspicuous places in said city, at least three days prior to the time of the meeting, which notice shall contain the substance of said estimate. Said meeting shall transact the business for which it was called. If a majority of the citizens present shall consent to the levying of the taxes specified in said estimate, then the Common Council shall proceed to levy, assess and collect the same, or such part thereof as may have been consented to; but if said meeting shall not consent to the levying of said taxes, the said Common Council may call a second meeting of said citizens in the same manner, and which shall have the same power as the first meeting hereinbefore provided for.

Public meeting to vote taxes.

Second meeting.

Taxes for Interest Fund.

Sec. 6. The Common Council shall annually levy, assess and collect on the assessed value of all the real and personal estate in said city, made taxable by the laws of this State, taxes for the purposes of the Interest Fund, not exceeding, in amount, a sufficient sum to pay the interest accrued or to accrue on the funded debt of said city, for the year for which such taxes are levied; and also taxes not less than five, nor more than ten thousand dollars, for the purposes of the Sinking Fund.

Special sewer tax.

Sec. 7. The Common Council shall also have power annually to levy, assess and collect a tax or assessment on all lots, premises and sub-divisions, thereof, drained by paivate sewers or drains, leading into or connected with any public sewer, or drain, which tax shall be one dollar and fitfy cents on every lot, premises or sub-division thereof having a cellar, fifty cents if there be no cellar thereon, and such sums as the

Common Council may fix for all lots and establishments drained as aforesaid, and requiring an unusual or extraordinary amount of drainage. Said tax or assessment shall be credited to the Sewer Fund, and applied to the repairing of sewers and drains, and if the same be more than is required for such purpose, the surplus may be applied to the construction of sewers and drains.

Tax for grading, paving, &c.

SEC. 8. The Common Council shall also have power from time to time to levy, assess and collect a tax or assessment on all lots, premises or sub-divisions thereof, sufficient to defray the expenses of grading and paving, gravelling, macadamizing or planking any highway, avenue, street, lane, alley, or cross-walk in said city, in front of or adjacent to such lots, premises or sub-divisions thereof, and of putting curb-stones and culverts therein, which tax or assessment shall be credited to the Street Paving Fund: *Provided, however,* That such tax or assessment shall not, in any one year exceed, in the aggregate, the sum of fifty thousand dollars; such grading, paving, gravelling, macadamizing and putting in of curb-stones and culverts shall be commenced and completed, and all contracts therefor shall require the same to be commenced and completed within the six months next preceding the first day of December.

Proviso.

Loans for Public Building Fund.

SEC. 9. The Common Council shall also have power to provide money for the Public Building Fund, by loaning, upon the faith and credit of said city, and upon the best terms that can be made, a sum of money not exceeding three hundred thousand dollars, and to issue the bonds of said city to an amount not exceeding that sum, pledging its faith and credit for the payment of the principal and interest, but said bonds shall not be negotiated at less than their par value. Said bonds shall be denominated "Public Building Stock of the City of Detroit," shall be regularly dated and numbered in the order of their issuance; shall be for sums not less than five hundred dollars each; shall bear interest not exceeding seven per cent. per annum; shall be payable in not lesss than twenty years from date; shall be issued under the seal of the corporation, signed by the Mayor, and countersigned by the Controller. The Controller shall keep an accurate record of said bonds, showing the class of indebbtedness to which they belong, the number, date, and amount of each bond, its rate of interest, when and where the same is payable, and the person to whom it is issued. The proceeds of said bonds shall be paid to the Treasurer, and be credited to the Public Building Fund, and applied exclusively to the purposes for which said fund is constituted as above; but the Common Council shall not expend for the purposes of said Public Building Fund in any one year more than fifty thousand dollars, nor issue in any one year a greater amount of said bonds than to the amount of fifty thousand dollars.

Contract for Public Building Fund not to exceed $50,000 in any year.

SEC. 10. No contract shall be let or entered into for labor or materials to be employed in the construction of a City Hall, building for the use of the officers of the corporation, alms house, jail, work house, house of correction, or market building, exceeding in amount fifty thousand dollars in any one year; and no bonds shall be issued as aforesaid for the purposes of the Public Building Fund, until a public meeting of the citizens of said city shall have been called and held to consider the subject of constructing a public building for such purpose as the Common Council may propose, which meeting shall be called and may be held in the manner above prescribed for calling and holding a meeting in relation to the levying of taxes. The Common Council shall cause to be presented to said meeting, by the Controller, an estimate of the necessary cost of purchasing the necessary real estate for the erection thereon of any building and expense of the building proposed to be constructed. If a majority of the citizens present shall consent to the purchase of such real estate, and construction of a building for the purpose proposed, and to the estimate presented, or any part thereof, the Common Council shall then be authorized to contract for the purchase of such real estate and for the con-

Consent of public meeting required for issue of bonds.

struction of said building, at a cost and expense not exceeding in amount, the estimate or part thereof thus consented to, and to expend thereon, borrow money and issue bonds as above provided, not exceeding fifty thousand dollars in any one year, nor exceeding the estimated cost and expense or part thereof consented to as aforesaid.

No contract to be made except as herein provided.

SEC. 11. No contract shall be let or entered into for the construction of any public work within said city, not herein otherwise provided for, and no such public work shall be commenced, until it shall have been approved by the Common Council, and a tax or assessment levied to defray the cost and expense thereof; and no such public work shall be paid for or contracted to be paid for, except out of the proceeds of the tax or assessment thus levied.

No contract for over $200 to be let except to the lowest bidder

SEC. 12. No contract for the purchase of any real estate, or for the construction of any public building, sewer, paving, graveling, planking, macadamizing, or for the construction of any public work whatever, or for any work to be done, or for purchasing or furnishing any material, printing or supplies for said corporation, if the purchase of such real estate, or the expense of such construction, repairs, work, materials, printing or supplies shall exceed two hundred dollars, shall be let or entered into, except to and with the lowest responsible bidder with adequate security, and as to such work or material, requiring mechanical skill, to and with practical mechanics, and as to such other work, supplies or material not requiring mechanical skill, to and with such persons as shall be deemed competent for the performance of any such contract, and not until advertised proposals and specifications therefor shall have been duly published in at least one daily newspaper published in said city, and for such period as the Common Council shall prescribe. And no bids shall be accepted from, or contract awarded to, any person who is in arrears to the corporation upon debt or contract, or who is a defaulter as security, or otherwise, upon any obligation to the corporation, or who shall be in other respects disqualified according to the provisions of this act.

Evidence of debt; for what issued.

SEC. 13. No loan, bond or other evidence of debt, not expressly authorized by this act or any act hereby continued in force, shall be made or issued by the Common Council or any officer of the corporation: *Provided, however*, That the Common Council may issue new bonds for the refunding of bonds and evidences of debt already issued; and the proper officer of the corporation may draw and issue orders on the Treasurer for the necessary and current expenses of the city.

Council may authorize Controller to borrow money.

SEC. 14. The Common Council shall not have authority to borrow, except as hereinbefore provided, any sums of money whatever, on the credit of the corporation, but may authorize the Controller to borrow from time to time on such credit, in anticipation of the revenues of the corporation for the current fiscal year, and not to exceed such revenues in amount, such sums as may be necessary to meet the expenditures under the appropriations for the curent fiscal year.

New bonds what to show and how issued.

SEC. 15. All new bonds, issued for the refunding of bonds and evidences of debt before issued, shall show the class of indebtedness to which they belong; be issued on the best terms that can be made; be regularly dated and numbered in the order of their issuance; shall be for sums not elss than five hundred dollars each; shall be issued under the seal of the corporation, signed by the Mayor and countersigned by the Controller. The Controller shall keep an accurate record, showing the class of indebtedness to which they belong, the number, date and amount of each bond, its rate of interest, when and where the same is payable, and the person to whom it is issued, and showing also what bonds or evidences of debt have been thereby refunded.

Controller to keep record.

Refunded bonds to be cancelled and destroyed.

SEC. 16. All bonds and evidences of debt, when refunded, shall be cancelled and destroyed by the Treasurer, in the presence of the Controller and a special committee of the Common Council appointed for the purpose. He shall record and keep an accurate description of all bonds and evidences of debt thus cancelled and destroyed.

Bonds void when issued contrary to this act.

SEC. 17. All bonds and evidences of debt issued, and all contracts made or entered into contrary to or not authorized by the provisions of this act, shall be absolutely void. The Common Council shall incur no expenses and create or pay no debt or liability contrary to or not authorized by the provisions of this act, and shall not appropriate or use the property or moneys of the corporation, except as authorized by and in pursuance of law.

No illegal claim to be paid.

SEC. 18. No claim or demand against the corporation shall be allowed or paid, or warrant on the treasury issued therefor, if the same be contrary to or is not authorized by law, and no additional allowance beyond the legal claim under any contract with the corporation, or for any service on its account, or in its employment, shall be allowed. No warrant on the treasury shall be drawn for any claim or demand for the payment of which there is no money in the treasury raised or received for such purpose, or after the fund constituted and raised therefor has been exhausted by warrants previously drawn thereon, or by appropriations, liabilities, debts and expenses actually made, incurred or contracted for, and to be paid out of such fund.

No warrant to be drawn when there is no money in Treasury.

No money to be paid from treasury except on warrant.

SEC. 19. No moneys shall be paid out of the treasury, except upon a warrant signed by the Controller, and approved or authorized by the Common Council in pursuance of law. Such warrant shall specify the purpose for which the amount thereof is to be paid with sufficient clearness to indicate the particular fund constituted or raised therefor, shall have endorsed thereon the name of the particular fund out of which it is payable, and shall be paid from the fund constituted for such purpose, and from no other.

What warrant to contain and how endorsed.

Claim to be accompanied by affidavit.

SEC. 20. No claim against the corporation shall be audited or paid unless accompanied by the affidavit of the claimant, (if such affidavit be required by the Controller,) that the service, labor or materials upon which such claim is based, have been actually rendered, performed or furnished; that said claim is justly due, and that no part thereof has been paid, except as to the credits, if any, set forth in the account therefor.

Drafts on funds limited

SEC. 21. The Common Council shall not by warrant draft or order on the treasury, or by any form of contract, create any liability or expense, for the payment of which any particular fund is constituted as above, to a greater amount in the aggregate for any one year, than the amount of moneys raised for and paid into such fund for the year. All warrants, drafts, orders and contracts payable under this act, out of any particular fund, and issued or made after the moneys raised for and paid into such fund shall have been exhausted by payments therefrom, or liabilities created and to be paid out of said fund, shall be absolutely void as against the coporation.

Officers not to be interested in any contract with city.

SEC. 22. No contract or agreement, written or verbal, to which the corporation shall be a party, or to which any officer or board thereof shall officially be a party, for the construction of any pavement, building, sewer, or performance of any public work whatsoever, or contract or agreement requiring the expenditure, receipt or disposition of money or property by the corporation, of any officer or board thereof, or creating any debt or liability, shall be let or entered into, either directly or indirectly, with any member of the Common Council or other officer of the corporation, either as principal or surety, and any such contract or agreement thus let or entered into shall be absolutely void.

No ordinance &c., to be passed at meeting at which it was introduced.

SEC. 23. No ordinance, resolution or proceeding of the Common Council, imposing taxes or assessments, or requiring the payment, expenditure or disposition of money or property, or creating any debt or liability therefor, and no other ordinance shall be passed at the same meeting at which it was introduced, unless by unanimous consent, or at a special meeting called therefor, and every such ordinance, resolution or proceeding shall be passed by yeas and nays to be entered on the record.

SEC. 24. The Common Council shall determine the fiscal year, and within one month after the end thereof, the Controller shall render to the Common Council a full, complete and detailed statement, with tabular lists, of all moneys received and expended by the corporation for the preceding fiscal year, showing on what account they were received and expended, to what funds they were credited, and out of what funds they were paid, and classifying each receipt and expenditure under its appropriate head. In such statement he shall also give, by tabular lists and otherwise, such general information as may be necessary for an understanding of the pecuniary resources and liabilities of said city and of the condition of each fund, and may make such recommendations concerning the same, as the interests of said city may require. The Common Council shall cause said statement to be published in the daily newspaper published by the printer for said city, and in such other paper or papers as the Common Council shall direct.

Fiscal year. **Controller's report.** **What to contain.** **To be published.**

SEC. 25. The Common Council and the Controller, or either, may at any time require from the various officers and boards of the corporation, and it shall be their duty to furnish, when required, and in such form as shall be required, full and particular estimates in detail of the expenses of their offices or departments for the current or next ensuing fiscal year, and also full and particular accounts in detail of their expenses for any past year or for any part thereof.

Controller or Council may require estimates and accounts from officers and boards.

SEC. 26. The Common Council shall have power to contract with any safe bank or banks for the safe keeping of the public moneys and for the receipt of interest, at a rate not exceeding that established by law, upon such moneys of the corporation deposited with such bank or banks and to be drawn on account current from such bank or banks by the corporation or proper officer thereof, and such interest shall belong and be credited to the Sinking Fund.

Money may be put in Bank.

SEC. 27. The Mayor, Controller and Chairman of the Committee on Ways and Means shall be a committee for the

Committee for negotiation of loans.

negotiation of all loans authorized by this act, except as to any loans to be made by the Controller, under the authority of the Common Council, as above provided; and a majority of said committee shall have power to make such negotiation, subject to the approval of the Common Council.

Taxes, to what fund credited.

SEC. 28. All taxes and moneys raised, received or appropriated for the purpose of any particular fund, shall be paid in and credited to such particular fund; and all taxes and moneys not raised, received or appropriated for the purpose of any particular fund, shall be paid in and credited to the General Fund, or such other fund as the Common Council shall direct.

Moneys how applied.

SEC. 29. The moneys belonging to the several funds of the corporation, and all taxes and moneys raised, received or appropriated for the purposes thereof, shall be applied to the purposes for which said funds are respectively constituted as above, and for which said taxes and moneys are raised, received or appropriated: *Provided, however*, That if, from any cause, there shall be at the end of any fiscal year a surplus in any other than the Public Building Fund, the District Road Fund for each ward and the Sinking Fund, over and above the actual or estimated cost of any work for which the money of any fund was specifically raised, such surplus shall be transferred and credited by the Treasurer to said Sinking Fund, at the end of such fiscal year, whenever there shall not be sufficient moneys therein to pay the outstanding funded debt of said city.

Proviso.

Moneys not to be transferred from one fund to another.

SEC. 30. Moneys shall not be transferred from one fund to another, and the moneys received and properly belonging to one fund shall not be credited to any other or different fund, except to the Sinking Fund, as above provided; but the Controller shall have the power to divide the several funds above constituted into Special Funds, to defray special expenses belonging to the same class of expenses, for the payment of which said several funds are above constituted.

Funds may be divided.

SEC. 31. The Mayor, Controller, Treasurer and Committee on Ways and Means, and their successors in office, by virtue of their offices, shall be a Board of Commissioners of the Sinking Fund. They shall, from time to time, upon the best terms they can make, purchase or pay the outstanding funded debt of said city, or such part thereof as they may be able to purchase or pay, until the same be fully purchased up or paid; and all bonds and evidences of debt thus purchased or paid, shall be delivered to the Treasurer, and shall become and be the property of the Commissioners of the Sinking Fund, and the interest thereon shall be credited and belong to the Sinking Fund; and whenever they cannot arrange for purchasing or paying the said debt, or any part thereof, they shall, temporarily, and until they can so arrange, invest the moneys belonging to said Sinking Fund in such securities, paying an interest of not less than seven per cent., as they may deem safe and advisable. Said Commissioners shall, from time to time, and whenever requested by the Common Council, make report of their doings, which report shall be made to the Common Council, referred to and filed with the Controller, and recorded by him in some proper book, to be provided for the purpose.

Board of Commissioners of Sinking Fund.

Duties of Board.

SEC. 32. Said Board of Commissioners of the Sinking Fund shall be a board of the corporation within the meaning of this act, and shall be subject to the provisions of any existing or future ordinances of said city relative to the Sinking Fund. They shall meet from time to time for the transaction of business, and may adopt rules of proceeding at their meetings. A majority of the whole board shall be a quorum for the transaction of business, but they shall not purchase in, or pay the outstanding funded debt of said city, or invest any of the moneys belonging to the Sinking Fund as above provided, except under a resolution for such purpose passed and approved by the vote of a majority of the whole board, and by yeas and nays to be entered of record. The Mayor, or in case of his absence, some member to be appointed by those

Meetings of Board.

Who to preside.

Secretary, his duty.

present, shall preside at their meetings. They shall appoint one of their members Secretary of the Board, whose duty it shall be to keep a true record of its doings.

Treasurer to have custody of Sinking Fund.

SEC. 33. The Treasurer shall have the custody of all moneys, securities and evidences of value belonging or pertaining to the Sinking Fund, and shall pay out the moneys of said fund only by order of the Commissioners, or a majority thereof, and upon the warrant of the Controller.

Pledge for payment of moneys borrowed.

SEC. 34. The faith and property of the City of Detroit shall remain pledged for the final payment of all bonds issued and of all moneys borrowed by authority of and in accordance with this or any other act of the Legislature of this State.

Officer converti'g money of corporation to be deemed guilty of malfeasance in office.

SEC. 35. If any officer of the corporation shall directly or indirectly appropriate or convert any of the moneys, securities, evidences of value or any property whatsoever, belonging to the corporation or any board thereof, to his own use, or shall directly or indirectly and knowingly appropriate or convert the same to any other purpose than that for which such moneys, securities, evidences of value or property may have been appropriated, raised or received, or to any purpose not authorized by law, he shall be deemed guilty of willful and corrupt malfeasance in office, and may be prosecuted, tried and convicted therefor, and on conviction may be punished by fine not exceeding one thousand dollars, and imprisonment in the State prison, jail of Wayne County, or jail of said city, not exceeding three years, or either, in the discretion of the court.

Punishment.

CHAPTER IX.

ASSESSMENT OF TAXES AND THEIR COLLECTION.

Assessor—term of office

SECTION 1. There shall be an Assessor appointed by the Common Council, upon the recommendation of the Mayor, who shall hold his office for the term of three years, and shall devote his whole time to the service of the city, in connection with the duties of his office, with power to appoint two assistants, and shall receive such compensation as the Common Council may determine. Compensation.

SEC. 2. The said Assessor or Assessors shall, between the first day of January and April in each year, assess all the real and personal property subject to assessment or taxation by the laws of the State, within the limits of each ward respectively of said city; and the said Assessor or Assessors shall so discriminate in assessing said tax, as not to impose upon the rural portions those expenses which belong exclusively to the built portions of the city; for which purpose the Assessor or Assessors may, in his or their discretion, distinguish in their assessments what properties are within agricultural or rural sections, not having the benefit of lighting, watering, watching, and other expenditures for purposes exclusively belonging to the built and densely populated portions of the city, and all lands within said agricultural or rural districts exclusively used for the purpose of cultivation, pasture, meadow, woodland, or farming, may in the discretion of the Assessor be assessed as farm land, at their cash value; and said Assessor or Assessors shall, within the same period, make out and complete the assessment rolls, one for each ward respectively, in books to be provided for that purpose by the Common Council, and to be delivered to said Assessor on or before the first day of January in each year. The action of the Assessor or Assessors shall at all times be subject to the correction and revision of the Board of Review and the Common Council of the City of Detroit, as provided for in the charter of the city. Duties of Assessor in making assessments.

SEC. 3. The Assessor, together with the two Aldermen of each ward of the City of Detroit, shall be and are hereby vested with the powers and duties of Supervisors, as provided by the laws of this State, not inconsistent with the provisions of this chapter, and said Assessor and Aldermen shall attend the annual session of the Board of Supervisors, of the County of Assessors and Aldermen to have powers of supervisors.

Wayne, in October, and all other sessions thereof, and shall represent the interests of this corporation in said Board.

Proceedings where lots lie in two or more wards.

SEC. 4. If any lot or lots shall lie partly in two or more wards, the same shall be assessed in the ward where the greater proportion of such lot or lots is situated, and the said Assessor shall describe all lands, tenements and sub-divisions thereof, subject to assessment or tax in said city, by referring to the number and section of the lot and the owner or occupant thereof, and if the number and section of any lot or the owner or occupant thereof cannot be ascertained, then by such description as such Assessor may deem proper; and if, by mistake or otherwise, any person may be improperly designated as the owner of any lot, tenement or premises, such assessment or tax shall not for that cause be vitiated, but the same shall be a lien on such lot, tenement or premises and collected as in other cases.

Assessor may demand list of owner or agent.

SEC. 5. The Assessor shall have power and authority to demand of every person owning or having charge, as agent or otherwise, of any property taxable in any ward, a list of such property, with such description as will enable him to assess the same, which demand may be made in writing, and by delivering the same to such person or by leaving the same at his place of residence with some person of proper years and discretion, and if the person of whom such demand may be made, shall not, within ten days thereafter, deliver to such Assessor a list of the property in said ward belonging to him or her, or under his or her charge, with a correct description of the same, or if he shall omit any such property in the list delivered, said Assessor shall have power and it shall be his duty to assess such property upon such knowledge or information as may be satisfactory to him, at its cash value and according to his best judgement and discretion.

Board of Review, its duties.

SEC. 6. Said Assessor shall make out and complete the entire assessment rolls for the respective wards, and after all the rolls have been completed, the said Assessor, together with the Controller, Treasurer, Attorney and Chairman of the Committee on Ways and Means, shall meet together on the first Monday of April in each year, in the Common Council room in said city and organize as a Board of Review, for the purpose of hearing complaints of any and all persons against any assessments contained in any of said rolls, and altering or correcting the same, as the majority of the board shall deem proper. Said board shall continue in session from day to day, from nine o'clock A. M. until twelve o'clock noon, for the space of two weeks, which period may be extended by order of the Common Council, not exceeding ten days, and any person considering himself aggrieved in the premises, may complain thereof, verbally or in writing, before the Board of Review, and on sufficient cause being shown by the affidavit of such person, or by other evidence, to the satisfaction of such board, they shall review the assessment complained of, and may alter or correct the same as to the person charged thereby, the property described therein, and the estimated value thereof. The concurrence of a majority of all the board shall be sufficient to decide any question of altering or correcting an assessment complained of. The board, or a majority of them, having completed the review and correction of their assessment rolls, shall respectively sign and return the same to the Common Council. The members of said board shall receive no compensation for their services, whilst acting on said board, other than their salaries, excepting the Chairman of the Committee on Ways and Means, who shall receive such compensation as the Common Council shall prescribe.

Board of Review to receive no compensati'n except chairman of Committee of Ways and Means.

SEC. 7. At the meeting of the Board of Review, as required by the preceding section, they shall have the same power to review, correct and equalize the assessment rolls of the several wards, which Supervisors now or hereafter may have by law to review, correct and equalize the assessment rolls of townships in the respective counties of this State.

Board of Review to have same power as Board of Supervisors.

SEC. 8. The City Clerk shall cause a notice to the taxpayers of said city, to be published in the daily newspaper published by the printer for the city, and in one other daily

Notice of meeting of Board of Review, how given.

newspaper published in said city, for two weeks prior to the time of the first meeting of said Board of Review, stating the time and place of meeting of said board, and the objects for which it will meet, and the length of time it will continue its sessions. Said notice shall be published in said daily newspapers, on each publication day thereof, until the expiration of the two weeks provided above for the sitting of said board.

Appeal to Common Council.

SEC. 9. The Common Council, after the expiration of said two weeks or extended period in which the Board of Review are to sit, as above provided, for reviewing their assessment rolls, shall, at its regular session, proceed to consider said assessment rolls, and any person aggrieved by the assessment of his property, and the decision of such Board of Review thereon, may appeal to the Common Council at said regular session. Every appeal shall be in writing, and shall state specially the grounds of the appeal and the matter complained of, and no other matter shall be considered by the Council. While acting upon said assessment rolls or appeals any member of said board may meet with the Common Council and make such explanations as they may deem requisite in any case.

Common Council to hear appeals summarily.

SEC. 10. The Common Council shall hear and determine all appeals in a summary manner, and correct any errors which they may discover in the assessment rolls, and may place thereon the names of any persons and the descriptions of any property not already assessed, and assess the same, and may increase or diminish any assessment as they may see fit: *Provided*, That they shall not increase any assessment of property without giving a reasonable opportunity to the persons owning or having charge of the same, if known, to appear and object thereto.

Proviso.

Hearing appeals may be continued.

SEC. 11. The Common Council may continue the consideration of said assessment rolls and the hearing of said appeals from session to session for a period not exceeding sixteen days after the time when they are to be first considered as above provided, and on or before the expiration of said period of sixteen days, they shall be fully and finally confirmed by the Common Council, and shall remain as the basis of all taxes to be levied and collected in the City of Detroit according to property valuation until another assessment shall have been made and confirmed as above provided for.

SEC. 12. After the assessment rolls shall have been fully and finally confirmed, as provided in the preceding section, it shall be the duty of the Controller to cause the amount of all taxes, in dollars and cents, authorized to be assessed and collected in each year, to be rateably assessed to each person named, or lots described, upon and according to the aggregate valuation such person and lots shall have been assessed in said assessment rolls or books prepared for that purpose, to be known as the tax rolls for each ward, in separate columns, showing the amount of highway, sewer, school and city taxes assessed to each person or lots in each year; and when said tax rolls shall have been completed, the Controller shall cause the same to be delivered to the City Treasurer, who shall give a receipt therefor and be charged therewith, and who shall retain the said tax rolls in his office until such day as shall be designated by the Common Council, but not exceeding sixty days in each year, and during which time any person assessed therein may pay the amount of taxes assessed against each person respectively to said Treasurer, who shall receive and give a receipt therefor, and mark the same "paid" upon the proper roll; and after the expiration of the time for the payment of taxes to the Treasurer, as aforesaid, the Treasurer shall then cause to be made out copies of the taxes remaining due and unpaid on such assessment rolls, for each ward, and warrants authorizing the collection thereof, together with such percentage as shall have been fixed by the Common Council, as compensation for the collection of such taxes or assessments, and to be stated in such warrants, may be issued and annexed to each tax or assessment roll, signed by the Controller, and under the corporate seal of the corporation,

Controller to make tax rolls.

Tax rolls what to contain.

To be delivered to Treasurer.

Taxes may be paid to Treasurer.

Treasurer to give receipt.

Treasurer to make out copies of unpaid taxes and warrants for their collection.

Warrant to be signed by Controller.

directed to the proper ward collector or collector of the city, as the case may be, and made returnable upon such day as shall have been designated by the Common Council, commanding them to collect from the persons named in their respective assessment rolls the assessment or taxes therein specified and set forth as due from such persons, and for such purpose, if necessary, to levy upon and sell the personal property of such person, occupant or lessee refusing or neglecting to pay the same, whenever and wherever the same may be found within the limits of said city, and to pay over and account for the taxes or assessments then collected, according to law. The Treasurer shall charge the amount of taxes remaining unpaid upon said rolls to the collector or collectors of said city, receiving the same respectively, and shall also take a receipt therefor. Warrants for the collection of taxes or assessments may be extended or renewed from time to time, as the Common Council shall direct.

Form of warrant.

Treasurer to charge am'nt of unpaid taxes to collectors.

Warrants may be extended.

Powers of collectors.

SEC. 13. By virtue of said warrants, the several collectors to whom they may be respectively directed, shall have power to levy upon the personal property of persons from whom taxes may be due, wherever and whenever the same may be found within the limits of said city, and shall sell the same in the same manner and with the same duties and powers of proceeding as now or hereafter may be provided by the laws of this State for the collection of State and county taxes by Township Treasurers or Collectors; and all moneys thus collected shall be paid over by the collectors to the Treasurer of said city, at such times and under such regulations as shall be prescribed by the Common Council.

Taxes and assessments to be liens.

SEC. 14. Every assessment or tax lawfully levied or imposed by the authority of the Common Council on any lands, tenements, hereditaments or premises whatsoever in said city, shall be and remain a lien on such lands, tenements, hereditaments or premises, from the time of making such assessment or imposing such tax until paid; and the owner or occupants of or parties in interest in said real estate shall be liable on demand to pay every such assessment or tax, and if there be default in paying the same or any part thereof, or if such person or persons be non-residents of said city, and goods and chattels cannot be found out of which to collect such assessment or tax by levy and sale as hereinbefore provided, it shall be lawful for said Common Council to cause a notice to be published in the daily newspaper published by the printer for the city for four successive weeks, requiring the owners or occupants of or parties in interest in such lands, tenements, hereditaments or premises to pay such assessment or tax, and that, if default be made in making such payment, such real estate will be sold at public auction, at a day and place to be specified in said notice, for the lowest term of years at which any person shall offer to take the same, in consideration of advancing and paying such assessment or tax with the costs or charges in the premises. **Notice of sale of lands.**

SEC. 15. If the owners or occupants of or parties in interest in such real estate do not pay such assessment or taxes, with the costs and charges, within the period above prescribed for the publication of said notice, then the said Common Council shall have power, without any further notice, to cause such real estate to be sold at public auction for the lowest term of years at which any person shall offer to take the same, in consideration of advancing such assessment or taxes, with the costs and charges, and to direct the execution of a proper conveyance and certificate of such sale to the purchaser thereof; and if such real estate shall not be redeemed within one year after such sale thereof, as hereinafter provided, the Controller shall, in the name and for the City of Detroit, execute and deliver to such purchaser or his assignee, a proper deed for the conveyance of such real estate, for the term for which the same was sold, which deed shall in all courts be *prima facie* evidence of the regularity of all the proceedings under which the sale was made and said deed was executed, up to the date of the deed; and any person who shall under such deed enter into any such real estate, and erect or place any build- **Sale of real estate for taxes for term of years** **Redemption.** **Controller to execute deed of real estate for term of years.** **Deed *prima facie* eviden'e of regularity of proceedings.**

Purchaser may erect buildings on premises sold and may remove the same within three months after expiration of term.

ing or building materials theron, shall have the right at any time within three months after the expiration of said term, or in case he shall be ousted before the expiration of such term by any person claiming adversely to said deed, then within three months after final judgment of ouster or ejectment, to remove such building or building materials from said real estate.

Redemption.

SEC. 16. When any lands, tenements and hereditaments shall be sold according to the foregoing provisions for the payment of any assessment or tax, as aforesaid, if the owners or occupants of or parties in interest in the same shall within one year after such sale deposit with the Treasurer of said city, for the use of the purchaser, the full amount of the assessment or tax for which such real estate was sold, and such interest as the Common Council shall prescribe, as hereinafter authorized, together with the amount of the costs and charges, then the term for which such real estate was sold shall cease and be determined at the time of making such deposit, subject, however, to the right of the purchaser, his heirs, executors, administrators or assigns, to remove any building or building materials as hereinbefore provided.

Taxes paid may be recovered of person who ought to pay the same in action of assumpsit.

SEC. 17. Any person in possession of any real estate at the time any tax is to be collected, shall be liable to pay the tax imposed thereon, and in case any other person, by agreement or otherwise, ought to pay such tax or any part thereof, the person in possession who shall pay the same, may recover the amount paid from the person who ought to have paid the same, in an action of assumpsit, as for monies paid out and expended for his use and benefit.

Interest on Redemption.

SEC. 18. The Common Council shall have power to charge interest at a rate not exceeding fifteen per cent. per annum after the return of any assessment or tax, and twenty-five per cent. per annum, from the time of sale, on the amount of any assessment or tax, for the non-payment of which any lands, tenements or hereditaments may be sold, and upon the amount to be paid upon the redemption of any such real estate and premises so sold.

SEC. 19. Any person who shall at such sale purchase for a term of years any lots, grounds or wharves, shall have the right to remove any building or building materials erected or deposited by or belonging to him, and situated on said lots, grounds or wharves, at any time within three months after the expiration of the term or time for which the same were sold.

Right to remove buildings.

SEC. 20. The Controller, or in his absence the Mayor, may execute, in the name of the corporation and under its corporate seal, proper conveyances or certificates of sale of all lands, tenements, or hereditaments sold for assessments or taxes, which, when duly acknowledged and attested by the City Clerk, may be recorded as other conveyances of land under the laws of this State.

Controller or Mayor may execute conveyances.

SEC. 21. It shall be the duty of the Controller to bid in for the corporation at any sale of real estate for assessments or taxes every lot of land or premises, for which no person shall offer to bid, and if any purchaser shall refuse or neglect to pay the sum or sums bid by him within the time and under the regulations prescribed by the Common Council, such bid shall enure to the use and benefit of the corporation, if the Common Council so elect. Upon all such bids by the Controller and all bids enuring as aforesaid to the use and benefit of the corporation, conveyances and certificates of sale may be executed by the Controller to the corporation, acknowledged and attested by the City Clerk, and recorded in the same manner as above provided in other cases of sale for assessments or taxes.

Controller may bid lands in for city.

SEC. 22. All conveyances, certificates of sale and leases of any lands, tenements or hereditaments, executed by the corporation or any of its officers by virtue of this act, shall be taken and received in all courts and proceedings as *prima facie* evidence of the regularity of the proceedings on which such conveyances, certificates of sale, lease, or any title claimed thereby, are founded.

Conveyance to be *prima facie* evidence.

CHAPTER X.

FIRE DEPARTMENT.

Common Council to buy engines, &c.

SECTION 1. The Common Council shall procure fire engines, hose, hooks, ladders and other apparatus and implements used for the extinguishment of fires, for each fire company, pay the expenses of keeping the same in necessary repair, have charge and control of the same, and provide fit and secure engine houses and other places for keeping and preserving the same, and purchase any real estate for the erection of engine houses.

To organize Fire companies.

SEC. 2. The Common Council shall have power to organize engine, hook, hose, ladder, axe and other fire companies, for the prevention and extinguishment of fires, and to dissolve or disband the same; to appoint a competent number of able inhabitants of the City of Detroit firemen, to take the care and management of engines, hose, ladders and other apparatus and implements used and provided for the prevention and extinguishment of fires; to prescribe the duties and powers of firemen and fire companies, make rules and regulations for their government, impose reasonable fines, penalties and forfeitures upon them for a violation of the same, and to remove them for incapacity, neglect of duty or misconduct.

Chief Engineer and Assistants.

SEC. 3. There shall be a Chief Engineer and two or more Assistant Engineers, who shall be appointed by the firemen with the consent and confirmation of the Common Council, and whose powers and duties shall be prescribed by said Council.

Fire Wardens

SEC. 4. The Mayor, members of the Common Council, Marshall and Deputy Marshals, by virtue of their offices, shall be Fire Wardens, and the Common Council may annually appoint one or more resident electors of each ward, Fire Wardens thereof, who shall hold office until removed, or their successors be appointed and qualified.

SEC. 5. Each fire company shall have power to appoint its own officers, make by-laws and regulations for its good government, not inconsistent with this act or the ordinances and regulations of the Common Council, and may impose and collect such fines for the non-attendance or neglect of duty of any of its members, as may be prescribed by the by-laws or regulations of said company, and it shall be the duty of each fire company, subject to the control and regulations of the Common Council, to take the care and management of the fire engine, hose, hook, ladder and other fire apparatus and implements of such company, to keep the same in good and perfect repair, and upon any fire alarm or breaking out of any fire within said city, it shall be the duty of each member of a fire company forthwith to repair to the engine house of such company and thence proceed, without delay, with its engine, hose or other fire apparatus and implements to the place of such fire, and there use the same and otherwise labor for the extinguishment of such fire, under the direction of the Chief Engineer or other officers present, who may be empowered by the Common Council to give orders and directions at a fire in relation to the extinguishment thereof. Powers and duties of Fire Companies and Firemen.

SEC. 6. It shall also be the duty of each fire company to assemble once in each month, or as often as may be directed by the Common Council, for the purpose of working and examining its engine, hose or other fire apparatus and implements, and putting and keeping them in perfect order and repair. Meetings of Companies.

SEC. 7. The Fire Wardens appointed for the several wards, shall have power, at all reasonable times, and it shall be their duty to enter into and examine all the dwelling-houses, out-houses, lots and yards in their respective wards; to ascertain how ashes are kept; to direct full obedience to all ordinances of the Common Council, relating to the prevention of fires, and to report to the Common Council all infractions thereof; and the Mayor, members of the Common Council, Powers and duties of Fire Wardens.

Marshal and Deputy Marshals, acting as Fire Wardens, shall have the same powers and perform the same duties within the limits of said city which the appointed Fire Wardens may have and perform within the limits of their respective wards.

Exemption of Firemen.

SEC. 8. Every person, whilst serving as fireman, or who shall have served as fireman in said city for a term of five years, shall be exempted from serving as a juror and from doing militia duty, except in case of war, invasion or insurrection. A certificate of such service, under the seal of the corporation, signed by the Mayor and Clerk of the city, or as prescribed in the act incorporating "The Fire Department of the City of Detroit," approved February 14th, 1840, shall be, in all courts and places, evidence of such exemption. The Engineers, Assistant Engineers, Fire Wardens appointed for the several wards, and members of engine, hook, hose, ladder and other fire companies lawfully organized, shall be deemed firemen of said city within the meaning of this section.

Powers of certain officers at fires.

SEC. 9. The Mayor, any member of the Common Council, Engineer or Fire Warden may order all able-bodied persons present at a fire to assist and labor in the extinguishment thereof and in the preservation of property, and may also order all persons present at a fire, not belonging to the Fire Department or not lawfully employed in its service or in the preservation and custody of property, to remove from the vicinity of such fire all property exposed by reason thereof.

Power of officer at fire to arrest for disobedience of order.

SEC. 10. Whenever any person shall refuse to obey any lawful order of the Mayor, any member of the Common Council, Engineer or Fire Warden at any fire, it shall be lawful for the officer giving such order to arrest, or to direct orally the Marshal, any Deputy Marshal, Constable, Policeman or any citizen to arrest such person and confine him temporarily, until such fire be extinguished; and such officers or any of them may arrest or direct the arrest and temporary confinement of any person at such fire who shall be intoxicated or disorderly.

SEC. 11. Upon the breaking out of any fire within said city, the Marshal, Deputy Marshals, Constables and appointed Fire Wardens shall immediately repair to the place of such fire with their staves, and aid and assist in extinguishing such fire, and in removing, securing, preserving and preventing from being stolen, any goods or other property exposed by reason of such fire, and shall in all respects be obedient to the lawful orders of the Mayor, any member of the Common Council or Engineer present. Duties of officers upon breaking out of fires.

SEC. 12. Engine, hose, hook, ladder and other fire companies, now organized within the City of Detroit, shall be continued in their organization until dissolved or disbanded, and the present firemen, fire engineers and fire wardens of said city are hereby continued in office until removed; but said companies, firemen and fire engineers shall in all respects be governed by this act in respect to their powers, duties, liabilities, term and tenure of office, and by the ordinances, rules and regulations of the Common Council made pursuant to the provisions of this act. Present fire companies continued until dissolved or disbanded.

CHAPTER XI.

MISCELLANEOUS PROVISIONS.

SECTION. 1. The corporation created by this act shall pay and discharge all the debts, obligations, contracts and liabilities of "the Mayor, Recorder, Aldermen and Freemen of the City of Detroit," and suits may be brought and prosecuted thereon, against said corporation, in law or equity, to the same effect as they could be brought and prosecuted against "The Mayor, Recorder, Aldermen and Freemen of the City of Detroit," if this act had not been passed. New corporation to pay debts of old.

SEC. 2. All property, real, personal and mixed, and rights of property, in law or in equity, and all debts, fines, penal-

Rights vested in corporation under this act.

ties, forfeitures, rights and causes of action, and all rights and powers not inconsistent with the provisions of this act, which belong, have accrued, or may accrue, to "The Mayor, Recorder, Aldermen and Freemen of the City of Detroit," or to the inhabitants of the City of Detroit in their corporate capacity, shall be and the same are hereby declared to be fully and absolutely vested in the corporation created by this act, to be held subject to the provisions hereof, and may be prosecuted for and recovered or claimed, asserted and maintained by said corporation in its own name, or in any other lawful manner.

Actions pending continued.

SEC. 3. All writs, prosecutions, actions, and causes of actions, now in suit, and instituted or commenced, by or against "The Mayor, Recorder, Aldermen and Freemen of the City of Detroit," shall continue and may be prosecuted to the end thereof, to the same effect as if this act had not been passed.

Mayor's court continued until Recorder's court organized.

SEC. 4. The Mayor's Court of the City of Detroit, except as herein otherwise provided, shall continue with its powers and jurisdiction as if this act had not been passed, until the organization of the Recorder's Court under this act, and from and after such organization, its powers and jurisdiction shall cease.

Removal of records, &c., to Recorder's court.

SEC. 5. On the organization of the Recorder's Court, all books, records, recognizances and papers filed in or pertaining to the Mayor's Court of the City of Detroit, and all proceedings, commenced or cognizable therein, shall be removed and transferred to or commenced in said Recorder's Court, and proceeded with, in conformity with its powers and jurisdiction, to the same effect as if this act had not been passed.

Causes of action continued.

SEC. 6. All causes of action, rights and liabilities of individuals of the State, and of bodies corporate, shall continue and remain, as if this act had not been passed, except of "The Mayor, Recorder, Aldermen and Freemen of the City of Detroit," whose act of incorporation is hereby repealed.

SEC. 7. This act shall not invalidate any legal act done by

"The Mayor, Recorder, Aldermen and Freemen of the City of Detroit," or by the Common Council or any officer of said city, now or heretofore in office.

Certain acts not invalidated.

Sec. 8. All ordinances, by-laws, regulations, resolutions and rules of the Common Council of the City of Detroit, now in force, and not inconsistent with this act, shall remain in force until altered, amended or repealed by the Common Council, under this act, and after the same shall take effect.

Ordinances to remain in force.

Sec. 9. No person shall be an incompetent judge, justice of the peace, or other officer, witness or juror, by reason of his being an inhabitant or freeholder in the City of Detroit, in any prosecution or proceeding in the Recorder's Court, in any action or proceeding in which the corporation shall be a party in interest, or in any judicial or other proceeding.

Inhabitants of Detroit not to be incompetent.

Sec. 10. The certificate of the Clerk, required by this act, specifying the day on which he may have presented any ordinance, resolution or proceeding to the Mayor, for his approval or disapproval, or a copy thereof certified by such Clerk under the seal of the corporation, shall, in all courts, places and proceedings, be conclusive evidence of the facts therein stated.

Clerk's certificate to be conclusive evidence.

Sec. 11. The record of any ordinance enacted, and of the time of its first publication, made by the Clerk, as required in this act, or a copy thereof, certified by such Clerk, under the seal of the corporation, shall be presumptive evidence in all courts, places and proceedings, of the due passage of such ordinance, of its having been duly published, and of the time of its first publication. Copies of all other records and papers duly filed in and pertaining to the office of the Clerk, certified by him under the seal of the corporation, shall be evidence in all courts and places, to the same effect as the originals would be if produced.

Records or certified copies of records to be presumptive evidence.

Sec. 12. Proof of the requisite publication of any ordinance, resolution or other proceeding required to be published in any newspaper, by the affidavit of a printer or publisher thereof, taken before any officer authorized to administer

Proof of publication of ordinances, &c.

oaths and take affidavits, and duly filed with the Clerk of the City, or any other competent proof, shall in all courts and places be conclusive evidence of the legal publication of such ordinance, resolution or other proceeding.

SEC. 13. All ordinances and by-laws of the Common Council, printed and published by their authority, shall in all courts, places and proceedings, be received without further proof as *prima facie* evidence thereof and of their legal enactment and publication.

Perjury. SEC. 14. Any person required to take any oath or affirmation, or to make any affidavit or statement under oath or affirmation, under any provision of this act, who shall, under such oath or affirmation, in any such statement or affidavit, or otherwise, wilfully swear falsely as to any material matter, shall be guilty of perjury, and may be prosecuted therefor, and on conviction, punished, as in the case of perjury under the general laws of this State.

Public act. SEC. 15. This act shall be deemed a public act, and shall be construed benignly and favorably for any beneficial purpose therein intended.

This act may be amended. SEC. 16. This act may at any time be altered or amended by the Legislature of this State.

CHAPTER XII.

ACTS CONTINUED AND REPEALED.

SECTION 1. The following acts and part of acts being now in force shall be continued subject to this act, viz.:

The act entitled "An Act to incorporate the Fire Department of the City of Detroit," approved February 14th, 1840;

The act entitled "An Act to amend the laws relative to supplying the City of Detroit with pure and wholesome water, and to provide for the completion and management of the Detroit Water Works," approved February 14th, 1853;

The act entitled "An Act to authorize the Water Commissioners of the City of Detroit to loan money for the purpose of extending and improving the Water Works of said city," approved February 6th, 1855;

All acts and parts of acts relating to schools in the City of Detroit;

The act entitled an "Act amending an act relative to the registry of certain deeds, approved March 9th, 1844," approved May 7th, 1846;

The act entitled "An Act relative to conveyances in the City of Detroit," approved April 1st, 1850;

The act entitled "An Act to incorporate the City of Detroit Gas Company," approved March 14th, 1849, and all acts amendatory thereof;

Sections eight, nine, ten, eleven and twelve, of chapter one hundred and three, of the Revised Statutes of 1846, relating to the selection and return of jurors from said city, to serve in the Circuit Court for the County of Wayne;

Section forty-nine, of chapter thirty-five, of the Revised Statutes of 1846, relating to Boards of Health in cities and villages;

The act entitled "An Act to establish a Police Court in the City of Detroit," approved April 2d, 1850, and all acts and parts of acts amendatory thereof;

The act entitled "An Act to provide for draining certain low lands in the vicinity of Detroit," approved March 29th, 1849.

Sec. 2. The following acts and parts of acts are hereby repealed, viz.:

The act of the Legislative Council of the Territory of Michigan, granting a charter of incorporation to "The Mayor, Recorder, Aldermen and Freemen of the City of Detroit," and entitled "An Act relative to the City of Detroit," approved April 4th, 1827, and all acts and parts of acts amending or altering said act or charter, and not hereby continued; and all other acts and parts of acts relating to the City of

Detroit, and not hereby continued, the subjects whereof are revised and re-enacted in this act, or which are repugnant to or inconsistent with the provisions of this act.

Sec. 3. This act shall take effect immediately.

Approved February 5th, 1857.

APPENDIX.

AN ACT TO ENLARGE THE CITY OF DETROIT.

SECTION 1. *The People of the State of Michigan enact*, That from and after the passage of this act the following district of country shall constitute the City of Detroit, to wit: Beginning at the national boundary line in Detroit River on the continuation of the dividing line between private claims numbered 21 and 78, as confirmed by the Board of Land Commissioners of the United States; thence northerly along said dividing line to the southerly line of the Detroit, Monroe and Toledo Rail Road; thence north-easterly along said line to the present western boundary of the City of Detroit; thence northerly along said boundary to the north-western corner of said city; thence eastwardly along the present northerly boundary line of said city to the north-east corner of private claim number 14, known as the St. Aubin Farm; thence southerly along the line between said claim number 14 and private claim number 91, to a point where the northerly line of Leland Street, when extended in a right line eastwardly from the said city, would intersect the line between said claims; thence eastwardly at right angles with the side lines of said claims to the easterly line of private claims number 9 and 454; thence southerly along the line between private claims number 9 and 454 and private claims number 11 and 453, being between the farms known as the McDougal and Chapoton Farms, to the northerly line of the Fort Gratiot Turnpike; thence north-easterly along said northerly line of

Boundaries.

said turnpike to the easterly line of private claim number 15; thence southerly along the easterly line of said claim number 15 to said national boundary line; thence westwardly along said national boundary to the place of beginning.

Wards.

SEC. 2. So much of the above described district as lies below, or westward, of the present corporate limits of said city, shall constitute one ward, to be known and designated as the ninth ward of said city; and so much of said district as lies above, or eastward, of the present corporate limits of said city, shall constitute one ward, to be known and designated as the tenth ward of said city. And from and after the time above fixed for the taking effect of this act, the said district hereby annexed to said city shall be subject to all laws, ordinances and regulations which shall at any time be in force over the remainder of said city, and shall cease to be subject to the regulations or government of any other township: *Provided*, That the Common Council of the City of Detroit may at any time alter or divide the said wards in the manner provided by the Charter of said city for the regulation or alteration of the several wards thereof.

Proviso.

Election of Aldermen.

SEC. 3. There shall be elected, at the next ensuing charter election to be held in said city, two persons in each of said wards to serve as Aldermen, one in each ward to serve one year, and one in each ward to serve for two years, and the time of service for which each Alderman is elected shall be designated on the ballots cast for such officers respectively; and such other ward officers shall be elected at such election, as are provided for the other wards of said city, and the terms of office of all such Aldermen and officers shall correspond with those of similar Aldermen and officers in such other wards.

Other ward officers.

Place of holding Charter Election in 9th and 10th Wards may be appointed by Council.

SEC. 4. The Common Council of the City of Detroit may at any time before said charter election appoint the places for holding the same in the said ninth and tenth wards, and said election shall be conducted in like manner with those in the other wards of said city, except that, at eight o'clock in the forenoon of the day for holding said charter election, the electors of said wards present at the place of holding the polls shall elect, *viva voce*, three of their own number to act as inspectors of said election, who shall be sworn rightfully to discharge the duties of such inspectors, (which oath either of them may administer to the others,) and who shall be the legal inspectors of said election, and said inspectors in each ward may appoint one or more electors of each of said wards to act as Constables at and about the polls of such wards during said election day. **Mode of conducting election therein.**

SEC. 5. The Common Council may appoint any person to fill any office in either of said wards, which is provided for in the other wards of said city, (except that of Alderman,) and the officers so appointed shall continue to act, until their successors are elected at said charter election and are duly qualified, and no longer. **Persons may be appointed to fill ward offices.**

SEC. 6. This act shall take effect and be in force from and after its passage. **To take immediate effect.**

AN ACT to amend an act entitled "An Act to revise the Charter of the City of Detroit," approved February fifth, eighteen hundred and fifty-seven.

SECTION 1. *The People of the State of Michigan enact*, That section two of chapter nine of an act entitled "An Act to revise the Charter of the City of Detroit," approved February fifth, eighteen hundred and fifty-seven, be and the same is hereby amended so as to read, when amended, as follows:

SEC. 2. The said Assessor or Assessors shall, between the first day of January and April in each year, assess all the real and personal property subject to assessment or taxation by the laws of the State, within the limits of each ward respectively of said city; and the said Assessor or Assessors shall so discriminate in assessing said tax, as not to impose upon the rural portions those expenses which belong exclusively to the built portions of the city; for which purpose the Assessor or Assessors may, in his or their discretion, distinguish in their assessments what properties are within agricultural or rural sections, not having the benefit of lighting, watering, watching, and other expenditures for purposes exclusively belonging to the built and densely populated portions of the city, and all lands within said agricultural or rural districts exclusively used for the purpose of cultivation, pasture, meadow, woodland, or farming, may, in the discretion of the Assessor, be assessed as farm land, at their cash value; and said Assessor or Assessors shall, within the same period, make out and complete the assessment rolls, one for each ward respectively, in books to be provided for that purpose by the Common Council, and to be delivered to said Assessor on or before the first day of January in each year. The action of the Assessor or Assessors shall at all times be subject to the correction and revision of the Board of Review and the Common Council of the City of Detroit, as provided for in the charter of the city.

SEC. 3. This act shall take immediate effect.

EDM. B. FAIRFIELD,
President of the Senate.

HENRY A. SHAW,
Speaker of the House of Representatives.

Approved February 15, 1859.

M. WISNER.

STATE OF MICHIGAN, } SS.
OFFICE OF SECRETARY OF STATE. }

I hereby certify that I have compared the foregoing copy of an Act, passed by the Legislature of this State, in the year 1859, with the original, now on file in this office, and that it is a true copy thereof.

In witness whereof, I have hereunto set my hand and affixed the Great Seal of said State, at Lansing, this 5th day of March, A. D. 1859.

[L. S.] E. A. THOMPSON,
Deputy Secretary of State.

AN ACT to amend Section Three, Chapter Nine, of the Act entitled "An Act to revise the Charter of the City of Detroit," approved February fifth, one thousand eight hundred and fifty-seven.

SECTION 1. *The People of the State of Michigan enact,* That Section Three, Chapter Nine, of the Act entitled "An Act to revise the Charter of the City of Detroit," approved February fifth, one thousand eight hundred and fifty-seven, be amended so as to read as follows:

SEC. 3. The Assessor, together with the two Aldermen of each ward of the City of Detroit, shall be and are hereby vested with the powers and duties of Supervisors, as provided by the laws of this State, not inconsistent with the provisions of this chapter, and said Assessor and Aldermen shall attend the annual session of the Board of Supervisors of the County of Wayne, in October, and all other sessions thereof, and shall represent the interests of this corporation in said Board.

SEC. 2. This act shall take immediate effect.

EDM. B. FAIRFIELD,
President of the Senate.

HENRY A. SHAW,
Speaker of the House of Representatives.

Approved February 12, 1859.

M. WISNER.

STATE OF MICHIGAN, } ss.
OFFICE OF SECRETARY OF STATE. }

I hereby certify that I have compared the foregoing copy of an Act, passed by the Legislature of this State, in the year 1859, with the original now on file in this office, and that it is a true copy thereof.

In witness whereof, I have hereunto set my hand and affixed the Great Seal of said State, at Lansing, this 5th day of March, A. D. 1859.

[L. S.] E. A. THOMPSON,
Deputy Secretary of State.

AN ACT to amend the laws relative to "Supplying the City of Detroit with Pure and Wholesome Water," and to provide for the Completion and Management of the Detroit Water Works.

SECTION 1. *The People of the State of Michigan enact,* That Shubael Conant, Henry Ledyard, Edmund A. Brush, William R. Noyes and James A. Van Dyke be and they are hereby named and constituted as a "Board of Water

Name and style.

Commissioners for the City of Detroit;" who, and their successors in office, shall be known by the name and style of the "Board of Water Commissioners of the City of Detroit," and by that name shall have power to contract, sue and be sued, to purchase, hold and convey personal and real estate, to have a common seal, to alter and change the same at pleasure, to make by-laws and ordinances, and do all legal acts which may be necessary and proper to carry out the effect, intent and object of this Act.

Powers.

Seal.

SEC. 2. The said Commissioners shall hold their offices respectively for the term of three, four, five, six and seven years, from the first Tuesday in May, of the year one thousand eight hundred and fifty-three. Said Commissioners shall, within sixty days after the passage of this Act, decide by lot their respective terms, which decision shall be notified by a written statement to the Common Council of said city, which shall be entered of record on the books of the said Common Council; and at their first regular meeting in the month of April, in the year one thousand eight hundred and fifty-six, and annually thereafter, the said Common Council shall elect and appoint a citizen of said city, being a qualified voter and a freeholder, as a Commissioner, who shall hold his office for five years from the first Tuesday in the May next following: *Provided*, That this section shall not be so construed as to disqualify any member of the said Board for re-appointment. And in case of the death or resignation, or removal from the city, of any of said Commissioners, the Common Council shall, as soon thereafter as possible, appoint to fill such vacancy, for the remainder of the term, some citizen of said city, being a qualified voter and a freeholder.

Term of office.

Vacancy, how filled.

SEC. 3. The said Commissioners shall choose one of their own number as President, who shall hold his office until the first Tuesday of May next ensuing the date of his election; they shall also appoint some suitable person as Secretary, who shall hold his office at the pleasure of the Board. And in case of the death, resignation or removal from the city of

President & Secretary.

the President, the said Commissioners shall have power to fill the vacancy so happening as in the first instance.

Vacancy.

Power to loan money on bonds.

SEC. 4. The said Commissioners shall have power to loan, from time to time, upon the best terms they can make, after giving public notice by advertising in the city papers for sixty days, and in one paper in Boston and two in New York, for such time as they shall deem expedient, a sum of money not exceeding two hundred and fifty thousand dollars, upon the credit of said city of Detroit, and shall have authority to issue bonds pledging the faith and credit of said city for the payment of the principal and interest of said bonds, which bonds shall issue under the seal of said Board of Commissioners, and shall be signed by them, or a majority of them, and bearing interest not exceeding eight per cent. per annum. And it shall be the duty of said Commissioners to cause to be kept an accurate register of all bonds issued by them, showing the number, date and amount of each bond, and to whom the same was issued; and it shall also be their duty to cause to be furnished to the Auditor of said city a copy of such register, as soon as the same is made, which shall be preserved by said Auditor, and copied into the records of said city.

Registry of bonds.

Copy furnished Auditor.

Supply of water.

SEC. 5. It shall be the duty of said Commissioners to examine and consider all matters relative to supplying the city of Detroit with a sufficient quantity of pure and wholesome water, to be taken from the Detroit River, or such other source as may be deemed expedient, for the use of its inhabitants.

Power to employ Supts., &c.

SEC. 6. Said Commissioners shall have power to employ superintendents, clerks, collectors, assessors, engineers, surveyors, and such other persons as, in their opinion, may be necessary to enable them to perform their duties under this Act, and to specify the duties of such persons so employed, and to fix their compensation: *Provided*, That in no case shall said Commissioners receive, directly or indirectly, any compensation for their own services.

Commissioners not to receive compensation.

SEC. 7. Said Commissioners shall have power, and it is hereby made their duty, as soon as may be, after the necessary funds shall have been procured, as herein provided, to purchase such land and materials, and to construct such reservoirs, buildings, machinery and fixtures, as shall be deemed necessary or desirable to furnish a full supply of water for public and private use in said city.

Power to purchase land, &c.

SEC. 8. Said Commissioners shall have power to construct reservoirs, jets and fire hydrants, at such localities in said city as they may deem expedient and necessary, and to lay pipes in and through all the alleys and streets of said city; and also to construct in such localities as they may deem expedient, not exceeding one to each block, hydrants for public use, and to keep the same in repair; and also, with the consent of the Common Council of said city, to construct fountains in the public squares, or such other public grounds of said city as they may deem expedient.

Reservoirs.

Jets, Hydrants, &c.

Fountains in public squar's

SEC. 9. Said Commissioners shall, from time to time, cause to be assessed the water rate to be paid by the owner or occupant of each house or other building having or using water, upon such basis as they shall deem equitable; and such water rate shall become a continuing lien, until paid, upon such house or other building, and upon the lot or lots upon which such house or other building is situated.

Assessment of water rates.

Lien on premises.

SEC. 10. Said Commissioners shall have full power to make and enforce all necessary by-laws, rules and regulations for the collection of said water rates, either by the appointment of collectors to demand the same, requiring payment at the office, shutting off the water, or by a suit at law before any court of competent jurisdiction, or by sale of the lot or premises upon which such rates shall have become a lien: *Provided*, That such sales shall be conducted in the same manner, and shall have the same force, virtue and effect of sales of lots delinquent for city taxes; and *provided further*, That the attempt to collect said rates by any process above mentioned shall not in any way invalidate the lien upon said lot or premises.

Power to make By-Laws.

Sale of property for non-payment of water rates.

Record of proceedings.

SEC. 11. The said Commissioners shall cause to be kept an accurate record of all proceedings, together with a list of all assessments for water rates, which shall be subject to inspection at all times.

Report to Common Council.

SEC. 12. It shall be the duty of said Commissioners to make a report to the Common Council of said city annually, which report shall embrace a statement of the condition and operation of the works; a statement of the funds and securities of said Board, and all debts due and owing to and from said Board, together with an accurate account of their expenses; which statement shall be certified by said Commissioners, and shall be entered of record by the Clerk of said city, and published in such manner as said Common Council may direct.

Surplus f'nds to be invested.

SEC. 13. Whenever the receipts of said Board from water rates, or other sources, shall accumulate so that there shall be a surplus, amounting to a sum of not less than five hundred dollars, not needed for the payment of the current expenses or the extension of said works, it shall be the duty of the Commissioners, together with the Auditor of said city, who shall be associated with them for that purpose, to invest the same in some safe stock, or upon other real or personal securities. Such investment shall be made in the name of said Board, and in such manner as to make the same available for the payment of interest and principal of the bonds issued as aforesaid, as soon as may be. It shall be the duty of said Commissioners to pay the interest on such bonds, and as fast as such surplus fund will permit, also the principal as the bonds become due, as funds for such purpose shall, from time to time, accumulate. The said Commissioners may, when they have funds for that purpose, purchase the bonds so issued as aforesaid, whether the same have become due or not; and in case the said Commissioners shall at any time not have funds on hand sufficient to meet any of the said bonds at the time when they shall become due, they shall have the right to issue new bonds, for such

Payment of bonds and interest.

Purchase of bonds.

New bonds may be issued.

amount and on such time as they shall deem expedient, in the place of bonds so becoming due as aforesaid; the said old bonds to be cancelled in the registry thereof, and the said new bonds to be recorded in the manner hereinbefore provided. Old bonds cancelled & new bonds registered.

SEC. 14. Before entering upon the duties of their office, said Commissioners shall each take and file with the City Clerk an oath or affirmation similar to that provided in the case of other officers of said city. Oath of commissioners.

SEC. 15. All materials, procured or partially procured, under a contract with the Commissioners, shall be exempt from execution; but it shall be the duty of the Commissioners to pay the money due for such materials to the judgment creditor of the contractor, under whose execution such material might otherwise have been sold, upon his producing to them due proof that his execution would have so attached, and such payment shall be held a valid payment on the contract. Materials exempt from execution.

SEC. 16. Any member of said Board of Commissioners may at any time be removed by a vote of two-thirds of the members elect of the Common Council of said city, for sufficient cause, and the proceedings in that behalf shall be entered on their journal: *Provided*, That the said Common Council shall previously cause a copy of the charges preferred against the Commissioner sought to be removed, and notice of the time and place of hearing the same, to be served on him ten days at least previous to the time so assigned; and in case of such removal, the Common Council shall, at their first regular meeting, or as soon thereafter as may be, appoint some person, being a citizen and a freeholder, to fill such vacancy; and the person so appointed to fill such vacancy, may continue in office for the period his predecessor had to serve. Commissioners may be removed. Copy of charges to be served. Vacancy to be filled.

SEC. 17. The said Commissioners, and, under their direction, their agents, servants, and workmen, are hereby authorized to enter upon any land or water for the purpose of mak- Power to enter upon land or water.

15

ing surveys, and to agree with the owner of any property which may be required for the purposes of this Act, as to the amount of compensation to be paid to said owner.

In case of disagreement judge of court to appoint appraisers.

SEC. 18. In cases of disagreement between the Commissioners and the owner of any property which may be required for the said purposes, or affected by any operation connected therewith, as to the amount of compensation to be paid to such owner, or in case any such owner shall be an infant, a married woman, or insane, or absent from this State, the Judge of the Circuit Court of Wayne county, may, upon the application of either party, nominate and appoint three disinterested persons to examine such property, and to estimate the value thereof, or damage sustained thereby, and to report thereon to the said court without delay.

Confirmation by judge. Payment. Fee of property.

SEC. 19. Whenever such report shall have been confirmed by the Circuit Judge of Wayne County, the said Commissioners shall pay to the said owner, or to such person or persons as the court may direct, the sum mentioned in said report, in full compensation for the property so required, or for the damage sustained, as the case may be, and thereupon the said Commissioners shall become seized in fee of such property so required, and shall be discharged from all claim by reason of any such damage.

Payment when refused money to be deposited.

SEC. 20. And in case of the refusal by any owner or owners, person or persons, to receive such sums awarded to them for property required or damages sustained, then the said Commissioners shall deposit with the City Treasurer the sums so awarded, subject to the draft of said owner or owners, person or persons; and thereupon the said Commissioners shall become seized in fee of such property so required, and shall be discharged from all claim by reason of any such damage; and said City Treasurer shall keep strict account of all sums so deposited, and shall pay out the same on the drafts of the owner or owners, person or persons, to the credit of whom such moneys may have been deposited.

City Treasurer to pay on draft.

SEC. 21. If any person shall willfully do or cause to be

done, any act whereby any work, materials or property whatsoever, erected or used within the City of Detroit or elsewhere, by the said Commissioners, or by any person acting under their authority, for the purpose of procuring or keeping a supply of water, shall in any manner be injured, or shall willfully pollute the water, shall be deemed guilty of misdemeanor, and, upon conviction, shall be punished therefor as other misdemeanors are punished. Injury to property or pollution of water.

SEC. 22. If any person shall, without the authority of said Commissioners as delegated through any of their agents, perforate or bore, or caused to be perforated or bored, any distributing pipe, or main or log belonging to the water works of said city, or make or cause to be made, any connection or communication whatever with the said pipes or logs, every person so offending shall, for each offence, forfeit a sum not exceeding fifty dollars and costs of prosecution, to be recovered in the Mayor's Court of said city, or other court of competent jurisdiction. Penalty for boring pipe or connecting logs without permission.

SEC. 23. The said Commissioners, in their discretion, shall have power to extend the distributing pipes and mains, and to construct reservoirs, hydrants and jets, without the limits of said city; and to regulate, protect and control such portions of said water works without the bounds of said city in and after the same manner that they regulate, protect and control said works within said bounds. Power to extend pipes and construct reservoirs beyond limits of city.

SEC. 24. It shall be the duty of said Commissioners, at least thirty days before the time fixed by the Ordinance of said city for assessing city taxes, to make a special report to the Common Council of said city, what, if any, sum will be needed by said Commissioners, over and above the revenue of said Board, to meet the payment of interest or principal of the bonds issued as aforesaid; and it shall be the duty of the Common Council to raise said amount by a special tax in the same manner as general taxes, to be designated a water tax; and the said amount shall be paid over to said Board by the treasurer of said city. Com. to report to Com. Council what sum may be required to pay interest, &c. C. Council to raise sum by tax.

Commissioners not to be interested in contracts or purchases of materials.

SEC. 25. No one or more of the said Commissioners shall be interested, either directly or indirectly, in any contract entered into by them with any other person; nor shall they be interested, either directly or indirectly, in the purchase of any material to be used or applied in and about the uses and purposes contemplated by this Act.

Lands, &c., of present w'rks conveyed to Board of Com

SEC. 26. All lands, lots, docks, buildings, machinery, pipes, logs, hydrants, and all fixtures whatsoever, purchased, designated or used for the present water works of the said city of Detroit, are hereby conveyed to and vested in said Board of Commissioners, who shall have full power to regulate, protect and control the same; and all the authority, rights and power heretofore exercised and had by said city over said works, are hereby continued to and vested in said Board of Commissioners.

Power to make by-laws &c.

SEC. 27. The said Commissioners are hereby invested with full power to make and enforce such by-laws, regulations and ordinances as may be necessary to carry into effect the object and intent of this Act, and to supply any power or mode not already specified therein, and shall cause all such by-laws, regulations and ordinances, to be entered into a book to be kept for that purpose, and signed by the President and Secretary, which, when so entered and signed, shall be evidence in any court of justice.

By-laws, &c., to be entered in a book.

Acts repealed.

SEC. 28. All Acts or parts of Acts contravening the provisions of this Act, are hereby repealed.

Act amended.

SEC. 29. This Act may at any time be altered, repealed or amended.

Approved February 14, 1853.

AN ACT to authorize the Water Commissioners of the City of Detroit to loan money for the purpose of extending and improving the Water Works of said City.

SECTION 1. *The People of the State of Michigan enact*, That the Board of Water Commissioners of the City of Detroit shall have power to loan, upon the best terms they can make, and for such time as they shall deem expedient, a sum of money not exceeding two hundred and fifty thousand dollars upon the credit of said City of Detroit, and shall have authority to issue bonds pledging the faith and credit of said city for the payment of the principal and interest of said bonds; which bonds shall issue under the seal of said Board of Commissioners, and shall be signed by them, or a majority of them, and bearing interest not exceeding eight per cent. per annum. And it shall be the duty of said Commissioners to cause to be kept an accurate register of all bonds issued by them, showing the number, date and amount of each bond, and to whom the same was issued; and it shall also be their duty to cause to be furnished to the Auditor of said city a copy of such register as soon as the same is made, which shall be preserved by said Auditor and copied into the record of said city. And the said sum of money shall be expended by said Commissioners solely for the purpose of extending and improving the Water Works of the City of Detroit.

This act shall take effect immediately.

Approved February 6th, 1855.

I do hereby certify, the above and foregoing to be a true copy of an original act now on file in the office of the Secretary of State.

In testimony whereof, I have hereunto set my hand and affixed the Great Seal of the State of Michigan, at Lansing, this twentieth day of March, A. D. 1855.

ROD. R. GIBSON,

Deputy Secretary of State.

AN ACT to authorize the Water Commissioners of the City of Detroit to borrow money for the purpose of extending and improving the Water Works of said City.

Board of Water Commissioners may borrow money.

SECTION 1. *The People of the State of Michigan enact*, That the Board of Water Commissioners of the City of Detroit shall have power to borrow, upon the best terms they can make, and for such time as they shall deem expedient, a sum of money not exceeding two hundred and fifty thousand dollars, upon the credit of said city of Detroit, and shall have authority to issue bonds pledging the faith and credit of said city for the payment of the principal and interest of said bonds; which bonds shall issue under the seal of said Board of Commissioners, and shall be signed by them, or a majority of them, and bearing interest not exceeding eight per cent. per annum; and it shall be the duty of said Commissioners to cause to be kept an accurate register of all bonds issued by them, showing the number, date and amount of each bond, and to whom the same was issued; and it shall also be their duty to cause to be furnished to the Comptroller of said city a copy of such register as soon as the same is made, which shall be preserved by said Auditor and copied into the records of said city; and the said sum of money shall be expended by said Commissioners solely for the purpose of extending and improving the Water Works of the City of Detroit: *Provided*, That the said Board of Commissioners shall not contract said loan until they are authorized and empowered so to do by the Common Council of the City of Detroit.

Money, how expended.

Proviso.

This act shall take effect and be in force from and after its passage.

Approved February 10th, 1857.

SCHOOL LAWS of the city of Detroit, as collated and published by the Board of Education of said city, A. D. 1855.*

Detroit to be one school district.

SEC. 1. *Be it enacted by the Senate and House of Representatives of the State of Michigan*, That the city of Detroit shall be considered as one School District, and hereafter all schools organized therein, in pursuance of this act, shall, under the direction and regulations of the Board of Education, be public and free to all children residing within the limits thereof, between the ages of five and seventeen years inclusive.—*Act of* 1842.

Schools free to scholars of certain ages.

School Inspectors to be elected.

SEC. 2. In lieu of the School Inspectors now required to be elected in said city, there shall be twelve† School Inspectors to be elected in the manner following: at the next annual charter election, there shall be elected in each ward of said city, two School Inspectors, one of whom shall hold his office for two years, and the other for one year; and at every annual charter election thereafter, there shall be elected in each ward, one School Inspector, who shall hold his office for two years. No School Inspector shall be entitled to receive any compensation for his services.—1842.

Their term of office.

Not to receive compensation.

Vacancy in office of Sch'l Inspector, how filled.

SEC. 3. In case of a vacancy in the office of School Inspector, the Common Council of the city of Detroit may fill the same, until the next annual election, when, if such vacancy happen in the first year of the term of said office, the electors of the proper ward may choose a suitable person to fill the remainder of such term: *Provided*, The City Clerk shall give notice of such vacancy prior to such election, as may be required in other cases.—1842.

Proviso.

Persons elected Scho'l Inspectors refusing to serve, may be fined.

SEC. 4. Every person elected to the office of School Inspector, who, without sufficient cause, shall neglect or refuse to serve, shall forfeit to the Board of Education for the use of the library, the sum of ten dollars, to be recovered in an

*The figures at the end of each section refer to the year in which the several acts were passed.

For the laws relating to the "colored children" of the city, see session laws of 1841, page 48.

†By the increase in the number of wards of the city, the number of School Inspectors has been increased to twenty.

Proviso. action of debt in some competent court: *Provided*, No person shall be compelled to serve two terms successively; and the said Board shall make all necessary rules and regulations relative to its proceedings, and punish by fine, not exceeding five dollars for each offence by any member of the Board, who may, without sufficient cause, absent himself from any meeting thereof, to be collected as they may direct.

Board may establish, rules and regulations and fine its members.

Who to constitute Board of Education. SEC. 5. The School Inspectors, together with the Mayor and Recorder of said city, (who are declared to be *ex officio* School Inspectors,) shall be a body corporate, by the name and style of "The Board of Education of the City of Detroit," and in that name may be capable of suing and being sued, and of holding and selling, and conveying real and personal property, as the interest of said Common Schools may require; and shall also succeed to, and be entitled to demand all moneys and other rights belonging to or in possession of the Board of School Inspectors, or any member thereof, or any real and personal property or other rights, of any such district in said city; and the clear proceeds of all such property which may come into the possession of said Board, as last aforesaid, shall be expended and disbursed by and under the authority of said Board of Education, for the support of said schools, after paying all just and legal demands existing against the several school districts heretofore existing in said city: *Provided*, That said Board shall not be liable to pay an aggregate amount of indebtedness against any one district, greater than the amount received from the same by said Board.—1842, 1843, 1846.

Board a body corporate.

Its powers & privileges.

How proceeds of property received by Board to be disposed of

Proviso.

What a quorum of Board SEC. 6. The Board of Education (six members whereof may form a quorum,) may meet from time to time at such place in said city as they may designate. They may elect one of their own number President, and in the absence of the President at any meeting, a majority of the inspectors present may choose one of their number President *pro tem.*—1842, 1846.

Board to el'ct a President.

SEC. 7. The Clerk of the said city shall be *ex officio* Clerk of said Board, and shall perform such duties as the Board of Education may reasonably require. In case of the absence of said Clerk, or for any other cause, the Board may choose some suitable person to perform his duties, either as principal or deputy Clerk.—1842.

Who to be Clerk of Board.

SEC. 8. The Recorder of said city shall be entitled to a seat at the meeting of said Board, for the purpose of deliberation, and of acting on committees, but shall have no vote therein.—1842, 1846.

Recorder of Detroit may meet with the Board.

SEC. 9. The Board of Education shall have full power and authority, and it shall be their duty, to purchase school-houses, and apply for and receive from the County Treasurer or other officer, all moneys appropriated for primary schools and district library of said city, and designate a place where the library may be kept therein. The said Board shall also have full power and authority to make by-laws and ordinances relative to taking the census of all children in said city between the ages of four and eighteen years; relative to making all necessary reports and transmitting the same to the proper offices, as designated by law, so that said city may be entitled to its proportion of the primary school fund; relative to visitation of schools; relative to the length of time schools shall be kept, which shall not be less than three months in each year; relative to the employment and examination of teachers, their powers and duties; relative to regulation of schools and the books to be used therein; relative to the appointment of necessary officers, and prescribe their powers and duties; relative to anything whatever that may advance the interests of education, the good government and prosperity of common schools in said city, and (the) welfare of the public concerning the same.—1842, 1850, 1855.

General powers and authority of the Board.

May make by-laws and ordinances relative to certain matters.

SEC. 10. The Mayor's Court shall have jurisdiction of all suits wherein the said Board may be a party, and of all prosecutions for violation of said by-laws and ordinances.—1842.

Mayor's Court to have jurisdiction under by-laws of the Board.

SEC. 11. The said Board shall annually, in the month of February, publish in some newspaper of the city, a statement

Board to publish an annual statement.

of the number of schools in said city, the number of pupils instructed therein the year preceding, the several branches of education pursued by them, and the expenditures for all things authorized by this act, during the preceding year.—1842.

To establish a library.

SEC. 12. The Board of Education shall establish a district library, and, for the increase of the same, the Common Council are authorized annually to lay a tax on the real and personal property within said city of a sum not exceeding two hundred dollars, which tax shall be levied and collected in the same manner as the moneys raised to defray the general expenses of said city.*—1842.

Tax for, how levied.

Com. Council may levy taxes for support of schools.

SEC. 13. The Common Council of said city are hereby authorized, once in each year, to assess and levy a tax on all the real and personal property in said city, according to the city assessment rolls of that year, which shall not exceed two dollars for every child in said city, between the ages of four and eighteen years, the number of children to be ascertained by the last report on the subject, on file in the office of the Clerk of the County of Wayne, or in the office of the Secretary of said Board of Education, and certified by the President thereof; and the said tax shall be collected in the same manner as the moneys raised to defray the general expenses of said city. All said money shall be disbursed by the authority of said Board for the maintenance and support of said schools, and for no other purpose. The said Board of Education shall have authority to establish a high school in said city, and also to appoint a Superintendent of the public schools, under the charge of said Board, with such salary and with such powers and duties as shall be prescribed by said Board of Education.—1855.

How taxes collected and disbursed.

Board may establish high school, and appoint a Superintendent of public schools.

Who to be Treasurer of Board. His duties.

SEC. 14. The Treasurer of said city shall be the Treasurer of said Board, unless otherwise directed by said Board; he shall keep all moneys belonging to said schools separate from the moneys belonging to the corporation of said city, and he

* As to fines for library, R. S. 1846, chap. 158, sec. 25, 26.

shall not pay out or expend the school moneys without the authority of the said Board.—1842.

Duty of Collectors relative to school moneys.

SEC. 15. The Collector of said city, when he shall have paid any school money to said Treasurer or other person, shall take a receipt therefor, and file the same with the Clerk of said Board; and it shall be the further duty of the Collector, when he shall have made his final return concerning the collection of said tax, to make a report to said Board, stating the whole amount of school tax, the amount collected, and the amount returned by him to the Common Council as unpaid or uncollected. If any Collector shall neglect or refuse to pay to said Treasurer the sums of money required by his warrant, or to account for the same as unpaid, at the time and in the manner required by law, the Recorder of the city of Detroit, or the President of the Board of Education of said city, shall forthwith issue a warrant under his hand, directed to the Sheriff of said county, commanding him to levy such sums as shall remain unpaid and unaccounted for, together with his fees for collecting the same, of the goods and chattels, lands and tenements of such Collector and his sureties, and to pay the same to the Treasurer of said Board of Education, and return such warrant within twenty days after the date thereof.—1855.

Collectors refusing to pay moneys collected, how proceeded against.

Collectors & Treasurer to give bonds.

SEC. 16. The Collector and Treasurer shall, before they enter on their duties under this act, enter into such bonds to said Board, and with such sureties as may be deemed necessary, conditioned for the faithful discharge of their duties respectively under this act.*—1842.

Prior acts repealed.

SEC. 17. All parts of acts, so far as they relate to the city of Detroit, inconsistent with this act, are hereby repealed. And it shall not be necessary to elect any school district officers in said city, as heretofore required by law.—1842.

School taxes to be placed in separate column on assessment roll.

SEC. 1. That all taxes which have been or may hereafter be assessed and levied by the Common Council of the city

* See sec. 1 of act of 1846, cited on the next page, for further provisions relative to bonds of collectors.

of Detroit, under and by virtue of the authority conferred on said Council by the thirteenth section of an act, entitled "An act relative to Free Schools in the city of Detroit," shall be set forth in the assessment roll of said city, in a separate column, apart, and distinguished from all other city taxes; and that the Collector of said city shall collect, and is hereby authorized and required to collect, said taxes in money, and said Collector shall not be required or permitted to receive in payment of said taxes any liabilities or evidences of debt against said city.—1843.

What collector shall receive for school taxes.

Who to collect school taxes.

SEC. 1. That the Collectors of the city of Detroit, elected in the different wards of said city, shall act as Collectors of the school tax assessed and levied in said city in their respective wards, under and by virtue of the provisions of the act to which this act is amendatory; and that each of said Collectors, previous to his entering upon his duties, shall, in addition to the bond now required by law, make and execute to the Board of Education of said city of Detroit a bond with two good and sufficient sureties, to be by them approved, in the penal sum directed by said Board, conditioned for the faithful performance of his duties as such Collector; and that, in case of neglect or refusal of any one of said Collectors to execute and obtain such bond according to the provisions of this section, he be subject to a penalty of one hundred dollars, to be collected in an action of debt, which may be brought in any Court in this State at the suit and in the name of the said Board of Education of the city of Detroit. —1846.

Collectors to give bonds.

Conditions of bonds.

Taxes for building school houses and purchasing lots therefor may be levied.

SEC. 1. That in addition to the taxes mentioned in the act to which this act is amendatory, the Common Council of the city of Detroit is hereby authorized and empowered to levy and collect a tax not exceeding fifteen hundred dollars in any one year, to be expended in the purchase of lots in said city for the use of the public schools thereof, and in the erection and building a school house or school houses, with the necessary outbuildings and fixtures, on any lot or lots which may be so purchased, or any other lots now owned by the Board of Education of said city, or which the said Board may hereafter acquire: *Provided*, That said tax, when so levied and collected, shall be paid to the Treasurer of said Board of Education, and be vested in said Board to and for the purpose hereinbefore stated, and no other, and also that the title to such lots purchased shall also be in said Board for the purpose aforesaid.—1847.

Proviso.

Title to school lots in whom vested

SEC. 2. Said tax shall not be levied or collected, unless, at a meeting of the freemen of said city, called for such purpose as hereinafter provided, a majority of the freemen present shall assent to the same.—1847.

Freemen to vote on taxes for school houses.

SEC. 3. It shall be the duty of the Mayor, or Recorder, in case of the absence of the Mayor, or a vacancy in his office, to call such a meeting of the freemen of said city, for the purpose of giving their assent or dissent to such tax, when it shall be requested by petition signed by twenty-four freemen of said city: which call shall particularly express the object of such meeting, and shall be published in two of the daily newspapers published in the said city of Detroit, one week previous to such meeting: *Provided*, That the Mayor may call such meeting upon the notice herein mentioned, without such petition, at his own option.—1847.

Mayor or Recorder to call meeting of freemen to vote on taxes

Proviso.

SEC. 4. If the said Mayor or Recorder shall refuse to call such meeting upon the presentation to either of them of such petition, or shall neglect to do so for three days after the presentation of such petition, any two members of the Common Council of said city may, on the like petition, call such meeting upon a like notice and publication thereof, in the manner and for the time hereinbefore specified in the case of a call by the Mayor or Recorder. Such meeting may be adjourned from time to time by vote of a majority of those present.—1847.

Meeting of freemen may be called by two memb'rs of Council in certain cases.

SEC. 5. The said tax shall be levied and collected in the same manner as the tax provided for in the thirteenth section of the act to which this act is amendatory, and shall be

How taxes for school houses and lots to be collected.

consolidated therewith on the tax rolls; but it shall be the duty of the said Board of Education, in each and every year when such tax is levied and collected, to separate the amount thereof from the gross amount of money received by said Board for such year, and set it apart as a fund to be reserved for the purposes specified in the first section of this act.—1847.

Board of Education may borrow money and issue bonds for payment.

SEC. 6. The Board of Education of the city of Detroit is hereby authorized from time to time, on such term or terms of payment as they may deem proper, to borrow a sum of money not exceeding in all the sum of five thousand dollars, for the purposes specified in the first section of this act, at a rate of interest not exceeding seven per cent. per annum, payable semi-annually, and to issue the bonds of said Board in such form, and executed in such manner, as said Board may direct: *Provided*, That said Board shall issue no bond for a less sum than fifty dollars.—1847, 1850.

Proviso.

Bonds to be a lien on property of Board.

SEC. 7. The bonds issued under this act shall be a charge upon all the property of said Board, which shall constitute a security for the payment thereof: *Provided*, That no legal proceedings shall be instituted to enforce such lien, or to sell any property of said Board for the payment of the principal money of any of said bonds, until one year after such principal shall become due, according to the tenor and effect thereof.—1847.

Proviso.

Bo'rd to keep interest on Bonds paid and provide sinking fund to pay principal.

SEC. 8. It shall be the duty of the Board of Education, whenever they shall borrow any money under the provisions of this act, annually to appropriate a sufficient sum out of any money which may come into their hands, to pay the interest upon the same; and also in addition thereto, an annual sum equal to five per cent. upon the amount so borrowed, to be invested under the direction of said Board in bonds of the city of Detroit, bearing interest at such prices as the same can be purchased, to accumulate as a sinking fund for the payment of the principal of the sum so borrowed; both of which appropriations shall take precedence of all others.—1847.

SEC. 3. The removal of any member of the Board of Education of the city of Detroit, from the ward for which he is elected School Inspector, after such election, shall not operate to vacate his office; but notwithstanding such removal, any Inspector so removing shall continue to hold his said office, and to be a member of said Board, and all provisions of any act or acts which make such removal a vacation of said office, are hereby repealed: *Provided*, The removal of such member shall not be from the city.—1850.

Removal of School Inspector from ward for which he is elected not to vacate his office.

Proviso.

SEC. 137. Any person paying taxes in a school district in which he does not reside, may send scholars to any district school therein, and such person shall, for that purpose, have and enjoy all the rights and privileges of a resident of such district, except the right of voting therein, and shall be rated therein for teachers' wages and fuel, and in the census of such district, and the apportionment of moneys from the school fund, scholars so sent, and generally attending such school, shall be considered as belonging to such district: *Provided*, That a majority of the qualified voters attending at any regular meeting in the district in which such person resides, shall have determined that no school shall be taught in said district for the year: *Or provided further*, That such person shall not reside in any organized school district.—*Revised Statutes* 1846, *page* 235, *and S. L.* 1850.

Persons paying school taxes in any district may send scholars to the schools therein.

Provisos.

AN ACT in relation to Free Schools in the city of Detroit.

SECTION 1. *The People of the State of Michigan enact*, That in lieu of the ($1,500) fifteen hundred dollars mentioned in the (1) first section of an act approved March (12, 1847,) twelfth, eighteen hundred and forty seven, and in addition to all other taxes authorized by law to be assessed and levied for school purposes in the city of Detroit, the Common Council of said city is hereby authorized and empowered to

Com. Council authorized to levy taxes for building school houses

NOTE.—The State School money must be distributed on the first Monday in May in each year.—*R. S.* 233, *section* 119, *S. L.* 1847.

levy and collect a tax not exceeding ($20,000) twenty thousand dollars in any one year, to be expended in the purchase of lots and in paying for lots already purchased in said city for the use of the public schools thereof, and in the erection and building of school houses with the necessary outbuildings and fixtures, on any lots now owned by the Board of Education in said city, or which said board may hereafter require. Said tax, when so levied and collected, shall be paid to the Treasurer of said Board, and shall vest in said Board for the sole purposes hereinbefore stated; said tax shall be collected in the same manner, and with the same right, duties, powers, and obligations, as the general school taxes in said city.

Tax to be paid to Treasurer of Bo'rd of Education.

This act is ordered to take immediate effect.

Approved February 7, 1857.

AN ACT to incorporate the Fire Department of the City of Detroit.

Preamble.

Whereas, The members of an Association, known as the "Fire Department of the city of Detroit," have petitioned the Legislature to grant them an act of incorporation, to enable them the more effectually to accomplish the objects of their organization, and to provide means for the relief of disabled firemen and their families; therefore,

Fire Department of Detroit a body corporate.

SEC. 1. *Be it enacted by the Senate and House of Representatives of the State of Michigan*, That all persons who now are, or may hereafter become, members of the Fire Department of the city of Detroit, and their successors, shall be, and hereby are ordained, constituted and declared to be, and continue a body politic and corporate, in fact and in name, under the name and style of "The Fire Department of the city of Detroit," for the purposes recited in the above preamble, and by that name they and their successors may and shall have perpetual succession, and shall be known in law, capable of suing and being sued, of pleading and being impleaded, of answering and being answered unto, of defending and being defended, in all suits, complaints, matters, causes, courts and places whatsoever, and both in law and equity; and capable of having a common seal; of acquiring by purchase, gift, devise, or otherwise, and of holding and conveying any real, personal, or mixed estate, necessary, proper, or expedient for the objects of this incorporation: *Provided*, That the amount of said estate shall at no time exceed the sum of thirty thousand dollars.

May have a seal and hold real estate.

Proviso.

SEC. 2. The members of the Fire Department of the City of Detroit, hereby incorporated, shall have, and are hereby declared to have, full power and authority to make and prescribe such by-laws, rules, ordinances and regulations, and the same to alter, amend and change at pleasure, as to them, from time to time, shall seem needful or proper, touching the management and disposition of their funds for the objects aforesaid; touching the regular and special meetings of the Department; the regulation, duty and conduct of their members, delegates and Board of Trustees; the election and displacing of officers and delegates; the admission and expulsion of members; the filling of vacancies in offices; and touching every other matter and thing necessary or expedient for the good government and promotion of this incorporation, or which appertains to the business and objects for which the said incorporation is, by this act, instituted: *Provided*, That such by-laws, rules, ordinances and regulations, be not repugnant to the constitutional laws of the United States, or of this State.

May make by laws, &c.

Relative to disposal of funds. Meetings. Conduct of members and officers. Election of same. Admission and expulsion of members. Filling vacancies, &c.

Proviso.

SEC. 3. The officers of said Department by this act incorporated, shall be a President, Vice-President, Secretary, Treasurer, and Collector, who, together with the Chief Engineer of the Fire Department, and the delegates from the several fire companies, and other bodies, pursuant to the provisions of the Constitution and by-laws of the Department, shall constitute a board of Trustees, a majority of whom shall be a quorum for the transaction of business; and said officers and

Officers of Department.

Board of Trustees.

delegates, separately, and as a Board of Trustees, shall do and perform such duties and things as may be incumbent upon, or required of, them, by the constitution or by-laws of the Department.

Annual meeting of Fire Department.

SEC. 4. There shall be an annual meeting of the members of said corporation on the third Monday of January, in each year, at which the officers shall be elected by ballot, by a majority of the members present, from their own body. And the officers elected shall hold their offices for one year, or until others be chosen in their places; but in case it at any time happens that an election of officers shall not be made or had on that day, the said corporation shall not be dissolved, but it shall and may be lawful to hold such election thereafter, pursuant to public notice given in one or more of the newspapers printed in said city.

Names of officers for first year.

SEC. 5. Of the Fire Department of the city of Detroit, Robert E. Roberts shall be President; Frederick Buhl, Vice-President; Edmund R. Kearsley, Secretary; Darius Lamson, Treasurer; and Elijah Goodell, Collector; who, together with the Chief Engineer of the Fire Department, duly appointed by the Common Council of the City of Detroit, and the delegates chosen as aforesaid, shall constitute the first Board of Trustees, and shall hold their offices until the third Monday of January next, or until others shall be chosen in their stead.

Interest of funds appropriated to relief of indigent and disabled firemen and their families.

SEC. 6. The interest arising from the funds of the said corporation, except sufficient to defray incidental expenses, shall be appropriated to the relief of such indigent and disabled firemen and their families, as may be interested in the fund, and who may, in the opinion of a majority of the Trustees, be worthy of assistance.

Certificates, how obtained

SEC. 7. All certificates now required to be obtained by firemen from the Clerk of said city, pursuant to the provisions of any law of this State, shall hereafter be obtained from the Department by this act incorporated; which certificate, signed by the President and Treasurer of this Department, and countersigned by the City Clerk of said city, and under the seal of this incorporation, shall have the like effect of those heretofore obtained from the said City Clerk, and shall be satisfactory evidence of the facts therein contained. And each person applying for such certificate shall pay therefor such sum as the by-laws of the Department shall prescribe, for the benefit of the corporation and the objects thereof. Their effect.

SEC. 8. It shall be the duty of the Board of Trustees to make out and deliver to the City Clerk, once in each year, or whenever he may request it, an accurate list of all the members of this corporation, who are exempt from jury or military duty, that they are or may become entitled to the benefits thereof. List of members to be made out yearly and given to City Clerk.

SEC. 9. This act is hereby declared to be a public act, and the same shall, in all courts and places, be regarded benignly and favorably for every beneficial purpose hereby intended. This is public act.

SEC. 10. The Legislature may alter, modify, amend or repeal this act by a vote of two-thirds of each House. May be repealed or modified.

SEC. 11. All acts and parts of acts which contravene the provisions of this act, are hereby repealed; and this act shall take effect from and after its passage.—*Approved February 14, 1840.* Acts inconsistent herewith, repealed.

AN ACT to amend an act entitled "An Act to Incorporate the Fire Department of the City of Detroit," approved February 14, 1840.

SECTION 1. *The People of the State of Michigan enact*, That section 1 of an act entitled "An Act to incorporate the Fire Department of the City of Detroit," be, and the same is hereby amended, by striking out the word "thirty," in the last line, and inserting the word "sixty," so that said section shall read as follows:

SEC. 1. *Be it enacted by the Senate and House of Representatives of the State of Michigan:* That all persons who now are or hereafter may become members of the Fire Department of the City of Detroit, and their successors, shall be, and hereby are ordained, constituted, and declared to be and continue, a body corporate and politic, in fact and in name, under the name and style of the "FIRE DEPARTMENT OF THE CITY OF DETROIT," for the purposes recited in the above preamble; and by that name they and their successors may and shall have perpetual succession, and shall be known in law, capable of suing and being sued, of pleading and being impleaded, of answering and being answered unto, of defending and being defended, in all suits, complaints, matters, causes, courts and places whatsoever, and both in law and equity; and capable of having a common seal; of acquiring by purchase, gift, devise, or otherwise, and of holding and conveying any real, personal, or mixed estate, necessary, proper, or expedient for the object of this incorporation: *Provided*, That the amount of said estate shall at no time exceed the sum of sixty thousand dollars.

Approved February, 1859.

INDEX.

www.ingramcontent.com/pod-product-compliance
Lightning Source LLC
LaVergne TN
LVHW021409110826
845150LV00007B/1854